Big River
The Marginal Farm

Alexander Buzo

CURRENCY PRESS • SYDNEY

CURRENCY PLAYS Oct. 1989

General Editor: Katharine Brisbane

First published in 1985
by Currency Press Pty. Ltd.
P O Box 452, Paddington
N.S.W. 2021, Australia

National Library of Australia card number
and ISBN 0 86819 103 5

Typeset and Printed by Colorcraft Limited, Hong Kong
Cover design by Kevin Chan

To Malcolm Robertson

Robert van Mackelenberg and Diane Craig as James and Toby in the Melbourne Theatre Company production of The Marginal Farm. *Photo by David Parker*

Contents

Above: Diane Craig as Toby, Chris Connelly as Philip and Suzette Williams as Ellen in the Melbourne Theatre Company production of The Marginal Farm. *Photo by David Parker. Below: Merilyn Hey as Ivy, John Doyle as Evan, Margaret Johnson as Olivia, Vic Rooney as Leo and Julie McGregor as Adela in the Hunter Valley Theatre Company production of* Big River. *Photo by Harry Klopcic*

Searching for a Rock Pool

John McCallum

There is a moment in one of Alexander Buzo's early plays, *Rooted*, when the socially alienated protagonist Bentley returns from an early morning swim in a rock pool by the sea, and tries to tell his estranged wife, Sandy, of the peace he has found there. It is one of the few still moments in all the strident savage satire of Buzo's early plays, and it is a pointer to the personal search that all Bentley's dramatic descendants will undertake. Coralie Lansdowne (in *Coralie Lansdowne Says No*), hiding in her eyrie above the Pacific ocean; Edward Martello (in *Martello Towers*), on his island in Pittwater; Weeks Brown (in *Makassar Reef*), gazing down on the black sails on Makassar harbour — and now Adela Learmonth, in *Big River*, casting branches into the still waters of the Murray; and Toby, in *The Marginal Farm*, left almost alone on the island of Fiji — all of them are searching for the peace of Bentley's rock pool.

Bentley was surrounded by a nasty and shallow society, an oppression of which he was only dimly aware. The later characters (those, that is, like secret agent Maxwell Smart, who are 'allied with the forces of niceness') become increasingly conscious of their alienation from that society, and as they do, they leave it further and further behind. At first their retreat is angry and noisy — and not totally successful. Coralie lashes out at the three modern knights who set upon her in her den, but eventually she allows one of them to lead her back to 'civilisation'. Edward Martello finds his wife, Jennifer, from whom he has been separated, joining him in his retreat. The fact that their separation goes on the rocks gives them some strength to return to their old world. Weeks resists the telegrams calling him back to his successful but no longer satisfying job in Australia, but moves on to Washington, submitting on the way to a painful compromise with Beth, who ends the play humiliating herself and lying to him.

Adela's and Toby's retreats are more final, just as modern society is more firmly distanced from us by the historical settings. Adela is left high and dry on the banks of the recently-subsided river, as the new world of Federation sweeps all else before it. Toby remains in Fiji with her Indian lover and his Fijian mistress when all the other white colonials have departed. Adela and Toby may have found their uneasy peace, but we are not allowed to forget that the world outside is moving on — to become in time the world that oppresses Bentley and Coralie and Edward.

Nor are we allowed to think of Adela's and Toby's victories as easy or mindlessly escapist. Adela, throughout most of *Big River*, pursues her grim party-girl style as she battles to save the old world of her father, which she has once before rejected. Although there are plenty of times when we can see her vulnerability, she is tough and in the end she wins. Her triumph, though, is sad — not only because the old world is already dying as she wins it. She sits on the verandah, now mistress of *Wombelano*, pregnant, trying for the umpteenth time to mend her hoop (that great symbol of Victorian family life), and she says to the departing Charles:

> I've failed in my life. I've failed! I don't know what I was supposed to do, the example I was set was too vague, there were too many dreams without any point, but *this* I do know, about *this* I am not vague, I have failed. But one thing I want you to tell me, one thing alone. What was I supposed to do? *What was I supposed to do? What was wanted of me?*

The tone at the end of *The Marginal Farm* is even grimmer. If there is one thing that Toby has made clear, in her personal battle, it is that she does not want to end up a

... scatty dress shop lady, the sort of dress shop lady you see
with a violet shawl and nicotine stains ... who chatters along,
fairly inanely you'd have to say, and that's being kind, about
who's in town and doing what to whom. I would not like to end
me days like such a lady, a crone before her time.

And yet that is exactly what she has become, in her highly-
coloured clothes and her large earrings, when Ellen returns
at the end to visit her. Ellen listens for a while to her inane
chatter, then:

ELLEN: Oh Toby! Oh no!
    [*She runs out to the road.*]
TOBY: What was all that about?
ILLY: Never mind. Never mind.
TOBY: Was I being rude?
ILLY: No, Toby.
TOBY: It must have been something I did or said. Or
    maybe. Maybe it was the sight of me. Maybe that poor little
    girl came back to see someone exceptional. And what did
    she see? She saw me. Maybe it was the sight of me that drove
    her off. The sheer sight of me.

'If you go now you'll leave me in peace', says Adela to
Charles. Toby has less poise:

TOBY: They were both my children, you know.
ILLY: Yes, Toby. But now it's time to go.
    [*He escorts her into the house.*]

The history, in the plays in this volume, is vital — as, in
different ways, it is for a great deal of recent Australian play
writing. It is not history as treated in the early drama, with
its naively fictionalised accounts of Great Events and Great
Lives. (Buzo himself wrote an example of this in *Macquarie*,
relating Macquarie's struggles to those of embattled
liberalism in modern times.) Nor is it the vaudevillean
history of the sort popularised in *The Legend of King
O'Malley*. During the last ten years Australian drama has
incorporated history as an organic part of the action — as a
context without which the narrow psychological concerns,
or personal searches, of the characters remain trivial and
misunderstood.

The human characters in Patrick White's *Signal Driver*, for example, confront the spiritual world represented by the avatars, but they seek their spiritual fulfillment against the historical background of the great march of materialism in Australian society throughout this century. All of Louis Nowra's plays can be interpreted as complex (if sometimes annoyingly ambiguous) historical and political parables (such as *Inside The Island*, which recreates the history of British imperialism in Australia and ends with an allegory of the Gallipoli campaign). Stephen Sewell writes about European and recent Australian history, not from the point of view of the Great Historical Figures which, according to one theory, created it, but from the point of view of the ordinary people who live through it.

It may seem odd to place Buzo in this company. His roots are in the satirical tradition of the early 70s and his present concerns seem at times agonisingly personal. And yet *Big River* is clearly about the decline of a great Australian rural tradition at the turn of the century. All the imagery which so powerfully expresses Adela's personal attempts to recapture her past (like the declining estate, the indoor garden, and above all the mighty but still river itself) also expresses the historical movement towards Federation and the twentieth century. Nowhere else in Australian drama, or literature, is the coincidence of Federation and the turn of the nineteenth into the twentieth century used so powerfully. It is not a simple lament for the past, but it is an attempt to rediscover it — to remind ourselves of what we lost when we took being blooded in a European war as a symbol of national maturation. Maybe we were right to reject Captain Hindmarsh's great vision, but not to forget it altogether.

The Marginal Farm expresses another major historical change: the end of the old colonialism, and the realisation that Australia has done nothing to earn a place in the new Asian and Pacific world. This is Buzo's second play set in the geographical neighbourhood which we have not managed to make a cultural neighbourhood. In Makassar the Asian world is still exotic — a half-way house in which Weeks and Beth and Wendy and Camilla find some

temporary peace before journeying on to their respective
'Western' destinations. The fact that their journeys are,
respectively, to the north and south, is part of that same
geographical confusion which still allows us to refer to our
near north as South-East Asia.

In Fiji the tensions between the Indians and the Fijians
are more important than the declining presence of the
Colonial Sugar Refining Company. These tensions are the
product of Fiji's colonial history, the Indians having been
brought in to work the sugar fields. Now the colonialists are
pulling up sticks and moving out, leaving behind the
problems they have created (problems which remain to this
day, between the Fijian Indians and the original islanders)
and leaving behind also, as their contribution to Fijian
culture, Toby, a pathetic piece of Western driftwood in her
bangles and earrings. Again, this is not a lament for the past
(in this case it scarcely could be) but a reminder that it is
important to understand it.

These plays, then, end in a sad mood of compromise
because of the conjunction of the personal and the
historical. Their action shows the historical change but their
characters remain in the old time. From the point of view of
these characters' personal search for value, outside the
shallow society they have retreated from, the tone is one of
grim triumph. From the historical perspective theirs is a
sadly inadequate response to the new world.

In Buzo's writing, of course, (much more than with
White, Nowra or Sewell) the focus is most clearly on the
characters and not on the history. The smart, witty style for
which he became famous in the early 70s has matured into
an extraordinarily subtle and complex tool, weaving
together patterns of imagery, information about character
and thematic strands with a density which repays close
study. It is still witty, but the laughs have dropped away, as
the tone becomes more melancholy. Perhaps it is *too* subtle
for the simplicities of our major State theatre company
programming. (Both these plays have been remarkably slow
in doing the usual round of capital cities.) Like some of
Patrick White's stage writing, it is deceptively simple on the

surface. But there is no doubt that these plays will endure when some of the flashier works which are attracting comment have been forgotten.

Bentley, coming across his rock pool, stripped off and splashed around in the water sparkling in the sun. Then a group of early bathers came along and he hurriedly dressed and returned to his sterile 'unit' and his fatuous wife and friends, with disastrous consequences. Edward Martello and Weeks Brown also return, but they have hard-won allies to help them cope. Adela and Toby, having found their peaceful rock pools, never leave them. That is their grim victory, but by the end of their plays we have the overwhelming feeling that they have missed out on something. You might find peace in a rock pool, but you can't live a full and rich life there. The search that Buzo's characters undertake is still on — to find a place where you can.

Rock pools are too small. Oceans are too vast. The Murray is too placid. Makassar harbour and Pittwater came close.

Perhaps a lake.

Armidale, NSW, 1984

Reconciling the Inevitable

Aarne Neeme

These two plays stand almost like bookends, with
similarities in content, but facing opposite ways. Both deal
with the modification of hopes and expectations by the
circumstances of life; but while one moves toward success,
the other ends in disappointment. Though only half a
century separates their view of Australia, *Big River*'s theme
is unification, the rise of democratic rule, while *The
Marginal Farm* deals with dissolution, the decline of
paternalistic colonialism. In both plays the leading
character is a woman, whose fate is supported and shared by
her man; but while the men accept their situation, the
women continue to question it. They are the activists, the
rest are scattered to the wind.

Big River is about the start of a new world in which the
emphasis is moving from pioneering towards consolidation
and cultivation; from Captain Hindmarsh's navigation to
the 'care and growth of his family'. Federation is the background. In the foreground a family is brought together to
redefine their roles and responsibilities after the death of
their patriach (the old order). Their house, Wombelano,
is the beachhead they have reached.

In the course of the play all the characters are confronted
with the question of what to do with their lives; each faces
some crisis of doubt over their choice, which leads them to
question the expectations or avoid the decisions. Even the
old matriarch, Ivy, constantly regrets her position; but

despite all the mislaid plans and wrong intentions, the choices are inevitable.

The catalyst is the river, the life force of the play, whose resources are in danger of stagnation. Who will gain the inheritance and recharge the flow? Not the heir apparent, Charles, who is driven to take on the responsibilities; nor the tight-smiling Monica, who would sell it at the earliest opportunity; far less Ben, representing overseas interests; nor even Ivy, who never wanted it in the first place. It is to Adela the land belongs; her heart and energies are directed to conservation and nurture. Adela is strongly identified with the river — in her life and dreams she has always been running — but she has a vision of herself and the river being stilled. Throughout the play, the river has posed both a threat and a promise, the life force that can either quench or engulf. But the promise is kept — through irrigation, the Big River is tamed.

The play contains echoes of Chekhov's *The Three Sisters* (reinforced by its structural formality) in the Hindmarsh family's view of itself as apart from the townspeople. Adela does not want to mix with the excursion crowd, Leo at the outset is only tolerated by the family, and the celebration ball contrasts dramatically with the street-drinking of the vulgar 'townees'. But finally the Commonwealth of Australia is born through the marriage of the sons of convicts and the daughters of gentry (Leo and Adela); of the city and country (Hugh and Monica), and across class distinctions (Charles and Frances). The traditionalists, Ivy and Olivia, will end up in Melbourne; the new bloods, Hugh and Monica, have gone to conquer Sydney; and Ben, the real estate man, wants to enter Parliament.

Leo, the outsider who arrives without boots, shows that the Captain's boots do indeed fit him — he too is providing what is necessary for the survival of his own. Adela at last has shut a door behind her, but just as the full realisation of her father's death comes to her late, so does the realisation of what has actually happend to her by the end of the play. It takes Charles, whose incipient feelings for reconciliation have broadened into greater wisdom, to explain that one doesn't have to aspire to others' expectations, only to succeed in finding one's own level.

The Marginal Farm is also about growing up, breaking away from all kinds of paternalism. The background in this case is the last days of colonialism in Fiji; in the foreground Ellen and Philip are helped 'over the hill' into adulthood while Toby and Illy descend the slippery slopes of middle age. Growing is not always up, more often down, and mostly flat. Colonial Sugar Refining's colonialism basically benevolent, but one cannot cross it or be independent of it. It uses people only as long as they are useful and effects no reconciliation between the Fijians and Indians, but capitalises on the division. Marshal is the main authority figure, who automatically takes over from his first entrance, interviews Toby, pigeonholes problems, procrastinates behind procedures, delegates and finally assumes to himself all decisions. Illy rails against him, but Toby, like a good MCG (Buzo's acronym for middle-class girl), still defers to him about her future, even when she knows she has no need.

In this way the play displays the gap between teaching and learning. Toby teaches Ellen to grow up and move out, but she herself fails to learn the same lesson. Illy, similarly, does not profit from the advice he has sought. In George Bernard Shaw's words: 'Our conduct is influenced not by our experience but by our expectation of life'. Toby does manage to bring release to both her charges — giving the wilful Ellen direction and releasing the withdrawn Philip.

As in the shades of Somerset Maugham, which charter the decline of the Empire, outsiders can never belong; and living on the margin is a metaphor for the precarious claims they make on the land and each other. Marshal says: 'We're living on the fringe here. This is where our way of life ends and theirs begins. It's not "anything goes" here. If it's "anything goes" then we may well go.' Toby and Illy's relationship is on the margin; and ironically the alien status that disqualifies Illy from gaining his farm, qualifies him for the post of Field Officer. James is another contender for both Toby and the marginal lands. Though also an outsider, the difference in his approach is clearly seen in the

two ice-cream scenes, and the way in which Illy shoots down
James' suggested aeroplane jaunts with a 'slow mosquito'.

James is the harbinger of unfulfilled expectations.
Although his life has been 'a bit anti-climactic' — joining
the R.A.F. in 1946 — he nonetheless gives the impression at
first of being a principal character. In the course of the play,
however, he 'flames out' under adversity and lack of
application. James' goodbye is again the first of many and
while he leaves in bravado without his possessions, he still
clings to his 'bright young chap' image — like the Empire,
fading fast. In supreme irony, he wonders about Toby's
future. Ellen's expectations about her heroine Toby — 'such
guts, and what heart. And style too!' — are shattered by the
reality. The family expectations of Ellen and Philip are
dampened by the knowledge that the latter is engaged and
doing something with an electronics company in Hong Kong
and Ellen is being a glorified waitress in the sky. Even her
expected child causes little comment.

Again a sense of inevitability pervades the play — the
'Toby jug' is fated from the first to the last. Despite her
initial determination not to become a dress shop lady,
Toby's traits of 'spinsterishness' inexorably lead her on.
Ellen has expressed it earlier in the play: 'But if you *know*
that is the direction then is that a reason for giving up the
journey? Or is it the *journey* itself? Perhaps you know all
along what the result will be.' Neither Ellen nor Toby can
cope with a contemplation of the future. Ellen wants to cling
to an endless morning, while Toby is painfully aware that
there is in fact an afternoon; but she has found a new
country, and a new purpose — 'I feel so beautifully
balanced and innersprung' — so that she too is loathe to let
go.

Throughout the play the author makes us aware of the
wrong decisions being taken — how Illy's eye for the main
chance eventually traps him, how Toby, by maintaining her
small 'l' liberal stance and going public with Illy, ruins her
reputation and with it any chance of surviving even as a
'travelling governess'. In the end it is Taka who finishes on
top, because she is her own person, in her own place

exercising the Fijian expertise in politics (the art of the possible). Marshal, canny to the end, has got out at the right time with his 'NZ lass', while James has probably chosen Rhodesia as his next conquest — another doomed colonial bastion. Illy loses his edge, grows fat, and is reduced to hanging onto what remains. Toby takes refuge in becoming a 'local character', her vision diminished to the 'middle of the week', and reconciled to 'hurtling along, towards oblivion'. Ellen's reaction momentarily confronts her with what she has become, but she holds onto the hope that somehow things will improve 'in the daylight'. For Toby and Illy there is no second chance. The title ironically reminds us of their lost aspirations but also of the relatively unproductive terrain (neither mountains nor plains) they have inhabited.

It is vital to the understanding of Buzo's plays that nothing is irrelevant, everything has its significance. The language and symbols, ideas and images resonate through the plays and are totally cohesive. A small example from *Big River*: Hugh at the start hesitatingly declares an ambition to write short stories 'to express the energies of a new country'. By the end of the play he is writing a novel, *Walk Across the River*, demonstrating how he has grown in confidence, and venerating Adela and his newly acquired love of the river and all it stands for. In *The Marginal Farm*, Toby teaches from *Great Expectations*, which is telling enough, but even the alternate endings relate directly to the choices she and others have to make by the end of the play. Even more subtly, the *Richard II* quotation at the start of Act Two applies as much to Fiji as to England — a dear land divided into paltry farms, and lives threatening to disintegrate.

Buzo is a stylist: his plays are not slice-of-life naturalism, but rather heightened realism, a modern equivalent of poetic drama. He achieves this through an immaculate use and selection of language. John Sumner once said it required a Shakespearean actor to perform Buzo's plays; he referred to the precise placement of words, a feeling for rhythm and the ability to illuminate images. Consider the following speech by Olivia, beautifully balanced in

structure, as she slowly but indubitably veers off the subject
into her own private preoccupations:

> We're not ganging up on him and it's nothing personal. It's just
> that before Daddy got sick — not long before — I organised a
> dinner party for some navy people from Melbourne — they
> came up for three days and it was wonderful — just like years
> ago — and on the night of the dinner party — you should have
> seen the officers — absolutely impeccable, it was such a
> pleasure and I thought if only things could be . . . not that I've
> ever been unhappy here, although this past year . . . we've
> never really made friends around here . . .
>   [*Pause.*]

And the intricate rhythms of Toby's speech as she tries to
explain to Ellen something she is also realising for herself:

> Oow, it was nothing. No-thing. I was happy to be able to help
> out. But it's all different now, Ellen dear. Oh, yes. It's all
> different now. I think that, quick as a wink, and equally
> quietly, and with nobody there to see or push, I think that Illy
> and I, while nobody was looking, Illy and I might have just
> gone over the hill ourselves. Illy, I think, is certainly over the
> hill — look at the weight he's put on.

Actors need to establish empathy for such characters, by
presenting not just the surface glitter and cleverness for
which Buzo is known, but by explaining the very real
emotion beneath — i.e. the subtext, the vital source and
impulse behind the utterance. Buzo calls this playing
simultaneously on the line and under the line.

But Buzo eschews easy and conventional solutions. It
shocks us that Adela could consider herself a failure or that
Toby could end up as she does: we are programmed for
neater, more optimistic endings, and are confronted with an
author who strikes uncomfortably close to the bone. He
revels in understatement and irony, understanding that
although they may not be as spectacular tools as melo-
dramatic confrontation, by creating the right sort of inner
tension their effect can be far more powerful. Consider the
devastating simplicity by which the gravity of Charles'
injuries is implied in the final moments of Act Two of *Big*

River. Again in *The Marginal Farm* a number of confrontations are seemingly baulked at, none more so than when Marshal faces Illy and Toby, who are about to leave together for Sigatoka. Very little is said: what is implied speaks volumes.

Buzo also delights in using his properties symbolically. *Big River* opens with Adela bursting in, disrupting the slow stirring of the punch and causing red wine to be spilt over the tablecloth — thus demonstrating the impact she is to have on the play. Her next action is to straighten one of her father's maps on the wall, not as a matter of fastidiousness, but consolidating her connection with him. At the end of the act a smaller cloth is brought on which covers the table only partly: associated with Adela's reaction, it suggests a flag at half mast. The return of the silver knives marks Leo's acceptance into the family, while Adela's discarding her silver cigarette case suggests the beginning of her conscious commitment to Leo. The Captain's hat is passed on to Charles, then to Hugh, and the ubiquitous hoop is the magic circle of Adela's childhood which she tries to preserve. Act Four opens with two symbols of fructification: Adela's pregnancy and Leo's grapes, and it closes with Adela holding her hoop within the circle of her world.

His symbolism is subtler still in *The Marginal Farm*: each prop has been carefully chosen to reveal character or situation. We first meet Toby playing patience, holding herself at a distance from Lautoka. Gradually she lets herself go, until she becomes the gypsy lady. Each character gives such special signs: Illy pocketing the purse, Marshal taking a proprietary attitude to the orange juice Taka brings out for James, or passing on his legacy to Illy in aspirin. Ellen's neurotic dandelion, Philip's determined bowling and James' trying to arrange the toolshed as his own order falls apart. The washing being removed from the verandah coincides with Toby removing the obstacles within Ellen. The two chickens in the cage are Toby and Illy, and this present (or bribe) from Ram relates to the one Marshal is about to offer Illy. Petrol is power doled out by those who own it; it also becomes an aptitude test in measurement.

Finally Illy has 'just the right amount' to take out Toby in his car. Toby's apple for Ellen is both a reference to the witch (the one who used to be fairest in the land) and Snow White, and a reversal of the student/teacher relationship. Working on the Melbourne Theatre Company production, Taka putting the 'fat' padding onto Illy seemed a stylistic problem, until we found that she could assume an almost omniscient stage manager/chorus figure role between all the scenes in the play, and thus reinforce her casual supremacy.

Neither of these is a history play, nor a period piece. They are modern plays which use an appropriate setting to illuminate concerns which the author always sees in terms of the interrelationships of his characters. His method transcends the constrictions and inarticulateness of straight naturalism, and gives us a broader world picture and a compelling individual expression of emotion. Yes, emotion. For despite his early reputation of being cool-minded and hard-hearted, Buzo has developed a fine sensibility for revealing his characters' innermost fears and hopes, not just in the big moments, but in little ones. These are mature works, at once both humorous and moving, displaying great craft, wisdom and passion from one of our most accomplished playwrights.

Sydney, 1984

BIG RIVER

*The Melbourne Theatre Company production at the 1980
Adelaide Festival. Above: The Federation Ball, with
Liddy Clark as Monica and Mary Ward as Ivy; Les
Dayman, Robert Essex and Stewart Faichney as Leo, Evan
and Ben; and Sandy Gore as Adela. Below: Sandy Gore.
Photos by Jan Dalman*

Big River was first performed by the Melbourne Theatre Company for the Adelaide Festival at the Arts Theatre, Adelaide, on 7 March 1980 with the following cast:

ADELA	Sandy Gore
FRANCES	Clare Balmford
HUGH	Patrick Frost
CHARLES	Tim Hughes
IVY	Mary Ward
OLIVIA	Maggie Millar
MONICA	Liddy Clark
LEO	Leslie Dayman
BEN	Stewart Faichney
EVAN	Robert Essex

Designed by Anne Fraser
Directed by John Sumner

CHARACTERS

MRS ADELA LEARMONTH, thirty-six
MISS FRANCES PASCOE, twenty
MR HUGH CRANE, twenty-four
MR CHARLES HINDMARSH, twenty-eight
MRS IVY HINDMARSH, sixty
MISS OLIVIA HINDMARSH, thirty-nine
MISS MONICA HINDMARSH, twenty-two
MR LEO MULCAHY, forty-eight
MR BEN BROMLEY, thirty-four
DR EVAN LEE, thirty-six

SETTING

A large house outside Albury, New South Wales, on the banks of the Murray River. There is a front door on the right, an ante-room and staircase and a doorway leading to the rest of the house. In the ante-room there are chairs and a large table. Around the walls are framed maps. In the foreground on the left is the verandah, which has a swing seat.

The time is 1900, on the eve of Federation.

Act One: Wake in the Afternoon. October
Act Two: Spring at Wombelano. October
Act Three: Federation Ball. New Year's Eve
Act Four: A View of the River. May 1901

ACT ONE

Wake in the Afternoon

August 1900, late in the afternoon.

HUGH CRANE *stands looking at the framed maps.*

FRANCES PASCOE *stands at the table stirring a bowl of punch. She picks up a demi-john of red wine and begins pouring it into the punch bowl.*

ADELA LEARMONTH *pushes open the front door and comes in.*

ADELA: Hello, Frances.

FRANCES: Oh!

[*She spills some wine on the white tablecloth.*]

Oh no!

ADELA: Did I give you a fright?

FRANCES: I wasn't expecting you, Mrs Learmonth. They're all at the funeral.

ADELA: My train was late.

[*She takes off her wet coat and drops it on a chair, then straightens a map on the wall.* FRANCES *feels the stain on the tablecloth.*]

FRANCES: Mrs Hindmarsh will be so angry. She told me especially to use the white lace.

ADELA: Nonsense. Mother won't mind if you use another one.

FRANCES: But the only other one long enough and clean enough is the picnic cloth.

ADELA: Surely you can get one from the dining room, Frances.

FRANCES: The dining room table is round.

ADELA: Is it? Oh yes, of course it is. I remember telling my father once that I was sitting at the apex of the circle and he made some remark about geometry. Yes of course it's round. And all the cloths are . . .

FRANCES: Circular.

ADELA: Then use the picnic cloth.

5

FRANCES: Mrs Hindmarsh will be so angry.

ADELA: I'll handle that. I'll tell her it's fashionable at Government House.

FRANCES: She won't go along with that.

ADELA: Of course she will. She'll say, 'Do you hear that, Olivia? Picnic tablecloths are fashionable at Government House'. You'll be praised for your foresight.

FRANCES: But it's gingham.

ADELA: Good. That's ideal for a picnic. I will of course tell her it's my fault.

[FRANCES *starts moving the punch to get at the tablecloth.* ADELA *sits down and takes out a cigarette case and a long holder.* FRANCES *stops and looks up.*]

FRANCES: Welcome home, miss.

ADELA: Thank you, Frances.

[FRANCES *goes on with her work.* HUGH *comes forward.* ADELA *lights her cigarette. She considers* HUGH.]

Yes?

HUGH: I'm Hugh Crane.

ADELA: I suppose you're 'sorry to meet me on this occasion'.

HUGH: Yes. I'm a friend of the family.

ADELA: I *am* sorry. I assumed you were from the undertakers. I'm Adela Learmonth, a sage and mystic. I have an uncanny insight into human behaviour. Particularly my mother's.

[HUGH *grins.*]

HUGH: You're obviously able to sum people up at a glance.

ADELA: Oh, you sly-boots. You've seen through me already. Which branch of the family are you friendly with?

HUGH: I've been seeing your sister.

ADELA: Olivia?

HUGH: Oh, God no. Monica. I mean, Olivia's . . .

ADELA: Olivia's got her own following?

HUGH: She's a very nice girl. Woman.

ADELA: It runs in the family.

HUGH: I've heard a lot about you. Apparently you're a social secretary at Government House.

ADELA: For a week, yes. But now I have returned home. For

HUGH: Oh. Monica didn't say.

ADELA: I'll break the news to her gently.

HUGH: I'm sorry about your father.

ADELA: Yes.

   [ADELA *reflects for a moment.*]

HUGH: I only met him towards the end.

   [FRANCES *has removed the tablecloth. She holds it up.*
   There is a large red stain in the middle.]

FRANCES: Look at that. I'll be lucky to get rid of it.

ADELA: Soak it in brine, Frances, and please stop fussing.

   [FRANCES *takes the cloth out to the kitchen.*]

HUGH: You must have been close to your father.

   [ADELA *turns and looks at him.*]

   What I mean is, when Monica went in to see him he'd say,
   'Adela! Have you ever shut a door behind you?'

   [ADELA *looks as if she is about to cry, but then smiles.*
   HUGH *wishes he hadn't said that.*]

ADELA: Poor Monny.

HUGH: That was a crass thing to say.

ADELA: It's understandable. He was old and sick.

HUGH: No, I meant —

ADELA: I know what you meant. I used my insight.

   [*She stands and walks over to the maps.* HUGH *watches*
   her.]

HUGH: Your father drew those maps, didn't he?

ADELA: Yes.

HUGH: They're beautiful.

ADELA: Someone called him a consummate draughtsman. I
   think they were right.

HUGH: I wouldn't know about the accuracy. I was talking
   about the way they look.

ADELA: They're beautiful, accurate, and authentic. They're
   firsthand in every sense. My father explored all the
   tributaries of the Murray. All of them. Every creek and
   swamp and billabong. I went with him once. It was in
   flood time, when it was difficult to know what the river
   was really up to. Sometimes we could have been floating
   in the middle of a cow paddock. But they all turned out
   to be accurate maps. Even this one.

[*She indicates a map and peers at it.*]

Eighteen . . . Seventy-nine. How old was I then? Fifteen. Good God. Fifteen. And they have the gall to tell me I never grew up. What are you doing? Mental arithmetic?

HUGH: No. No, I was just thinking about your father.

ADELA: You can spend a lifetime doing that. The river people are very grateful to him. I remember when we first moved here the maps they used were just pieces of calico with charcoal marks. My father was called — deservedly in my view — a visionary.

HUGH: I suppose he was a navigator. When he was in the navy.

ADELA: He was a captain. Hence the name Captain Hindmarsh.

HUGH: Yes, of course. I meant before that. He was very successful, wasn't he?

ADELA: Successful? Yes.

HUGH: Why did he leave? Why come to Albury of all places?

ADELA: I suppose he just wanted to go inland. One thing I do know. He wanted to devote himself to the care and growth of his family. And his family reciprocated . . . after their fashion.

[FRANCES *brings in a bright red and white checked gingham tablecloth. She shakes it out.*]

Ah. Frances. Just the thing.

[ADELA *holds up the punch bowl and* FRANCES *spreads the cloth.*]

FRANCES: It's hardly suitable for a wake.

ADELA: Nonsense. All we need now is a dance-band. The object of a non-Catholic wake, Frances — and here I'm breaking new ground for you — is to focus one's thoughts on the future.

[HUGH *is studying the map* ADELA *had indicated.*]

HUGH: I can't see how you got around these little creeks in the *Werriwa*.

ADELA: We had a smaller boat then. They got successively bigger, like the dinosaurs. I always knew when we were about to get a new boat — or ship, as my father would say, just to be different. He would come in and sit down,

all grizzled and churned up and seemingly deeply
worried, and he would describe our current boat,
castigating everything from bow to stern, every feature
he'd praised when he bought it, every plank and bolt and
pane of glass. When he'd got to the end of this tirade he'd
pause and wait. And then Livvie and I would say 'We
need a new ship' and he'd pretend that was an original
idea and agreed with us immediately. Let's have some
punch.

[*The table has been re-set.* FRANCES *has picked up the
demi-john.*]

FRANCES: The punch isn't made yet, miss.

HUGH: Let me help you.

[*He pours the wine into the punch bowl.*]

ADELA: Careful. We can't afford another disaster.

FRANCES: It's all very well for you to —

ADELA: Absolutely. I'm sorry, Frances.

[ADELA *looks around the room, acclimatising herself,
then wanders over to the staircase and feels it.*]

HUGH: All right?

FRANCES: Thank you.

[*She takes the demi-john back to the kitchen.* HUGH
stirs the punch.]

ADELA: What on earth have they done to the staircase? This
revolting heavy varnish — it's like a plague. I thought my
beautiful *Wombelano* would be safe.

[*She looks around.*]

Still I can't complain. It's here to welcome me back. It
smells the same, of grapes and wax. The walls are
comforting, almost round, but perhaps that's an optical
delusion. The view of the river is quiet and grand. I
think, in fact, the river looks at its best when seen through
glass at a distance. And the green of the slope in the
foreground — it certainly plays its part. I think I would
die if anything happened to *Wombelano*.

HUGH: It'll be safe. It's been left to your mother.

ADELA: How do you know?

HUGH: Monica told me.

ADELA: I'm not addressing my brother-in-law-elect, am I?

HUGH: We'll see. You wanted some punch.

    [*He holds out a glass for her. She comes over and takes it.*]

ADELA: You must be a close friend of Monica's.

HUGH: We enjoy each other's company.

ADELA: Sounds very intense. Why didn't you go to the funeral?

HUGH: I'm a teacher at a one-teacher school.

ADELA: Really? How do you manage to keep order?

HUGH: [*sharply*] Why do you ask that?

ADELA: I just thought . . . a one-teacher school . . . with a single teacher . . . it could be difficult. Is that a sore point?

HUGH: No.

    [*Pause.*]

It used to be, in the city. But I'm on the road back.

ADELA: Oh good.

HUGH: I want to become a writer.

ADELA: Oh.

HUGH: I write short stories about . . . well . . . I want to express the energies of a new country.

ADELA: How terrifyingly worthwhile. I'm a philistine, you see. Just a party girl.

HUGH: You don't approve of my ambition?

ADELA: I think it's sweet. I think you're sweet.

HUGH: Sweet?

ADELA: Well, perhaps not. It's a figure of speech. But I want to tell you that any friend of mine is fair game for Monica.

HUGH: [*puzzled*] Oh.

ADELA: Short stories, eh? A writer.

HUGH: Monica doesn't mind.

ADELA: Apparently not. She seems to have taken you into her confidence on a number of wide-ranging issues. Has she told you what our mother intends to do with *Wombelano*?

HUGH: I think it's going to be business as usual for the time being.

ADELA: For how long?

HUGH: I don't know.

ADELA: The time being. How long is that? You're not much use, are you?

HUGH: What are you worried about?

ADELA: I'm worried about two things. I'm worried about me and I'm worried about everyone else.

HUGH: You seem to be sensing some kind of treachery.

ADELA: I can hold my own when it comes to treachery.

HUGH: Oh yes. You married without your father's blessing didn't you?

ADELA: Yes I did and you were informed of this glorious event by . . .

HUGH: Monica.

ADELA: Good. I like to see frankness in human relations. There's no place for below-stairs gossip in the world of tomorrow. Get me another punch, will you?

HUGH: [*doing so*] I'm sorry. I'm being presumptuous. This must be an awful day for you.

ADELA: Punch for a funeral. My father would have liked that.

HUGH: He specified it.

ADELA: Something else I didn't know about. If you're around long enough you'll see I'm always the last to know anything in this family.

HUGH: I hope to be around long enough.

[*She smiles at him.*]

ADELA: Good. I need an informant. Hugh, is it?

HUGH: Yes, but I don't know if I'm devious enough to be a good informant.

ADELA: I've got an idea you'll be a runaway success.

[*He smiles at her.*]

HUGH: I'll do my best. Actually, I'm looking forward to becoming part of this Hindmarsh family.

ADELA: So am I.

[*He stares at her. She brushes some dust off the map on the wall.* CHARLES HINDMARSH *bursts in the front door. He stops and looks around distractedly.* ADELA *goes up to him quietly and embraces him.*]

CHARLES: Hello, Della.

[*He wanders over to the table and pours himself a punch.*]

ADELA: I'm sorry I was late. Where are the others?

CHARLES: They're coming.

[ADELA *feels his coat.*]

ADELA: You're all wet. Charles, what have you been doing?

CHARLES: I ran on ahead.

ADELA: [*helping him out of his coat*] How was the funeral?

CHARLES: All right. Livvie got a bit upset. I want to go up to my room.

ADELA: Please stay here with me.

[CHARLES *hesitates.*]

Why did you run ahead in the rain?

CHARLES: I just wanted to get out of the coach. Livvie was crying. You know.

ADELA: I promise you'll be safe with me.

[CHARLES *smiles briefly and glances up the stairs.*]

Please don't go to your room.

[CHARLES *seems to accept this. He looks around.*]

CHARLES: Hello, Hugh.

HUGH: Charles, I'm sorry to . . . uh . . .

ADELA: He's sorry to see you on this occasion.

CHARLES: It's over with.

[*He finishes his punch and pours another.*]

How long are you down?

ADELA: See if you can guess.

CHARLES: A couple of days.

ADELA: Charles. Please. You're speaking of the old me.

CHARLES: Sorry. I think.

ADELA: You'll obviously never guess while you're so determined to brood about my past, so I'll tell you. For ever.

CHARLES: What, here? For ever?

ADELA: Yes. It is my clear, unqualified intention to devote myself to the care and growth of my family.

CHARLES: That's an impossible task.

ADELA: If I read your thoughts correctly, you seem to be thinking 'The family has suffered a loss and now it's in for a disaster'.

CHARLES: Don't be silly, Della. I think it's admirable. But what will you actually do?

ADELA: These things are intangible.

CHARLES: What happens if Mother tells you to go back to Sydney?

ADELA: Then I shall lash myself to the staircase and fight off all comers with a carving knife.

HUGH: You must admit you're embarking on an ambitious project.

CHARLES: When Adela says something, she means it. For at least five minutes.

ADELA: Charles, you're living in the past.

HUGH: Perhaps it's not my place to point out what might happen in the future, but —

ADELA: I won't hear it. I won't hear anything negative.

HUGH: I thought you wanted an informant.

ADELA: Yes, you're right. We do have a pact, don't we? Fire away.

HUGH: I was just wondering what might happen if your mother decides to sell the place?

ADELA: Don't wonder. An informant doesn't wonder.

HUGH: I'm sorry. I'll keep to the facts in future.

ADELA: Good. Now. For my first project. What are your plans, Charles? What will you do?

CHARLES: I just want to go up to my room. I'll see you in a little while.

[*He goes purposefully towards the staircase.* FRANCES *comes in with a vase of flowers.* CHARLES *stops.*]

FRANCES: Would you like something to eat?

[CHARLES *hesitates, looking at her.* IVY *and* OLIVIA HINDMARSH *come in the front door.*]

IVY: Charles! Why didn't you stop when I called you?

CHARLES: Adela's here.

IVY: Get us a drink. [*Advancing on* ADELA] Della darling.
[*They embrace.*]
I could have bet money, you know. I knew you wouldn't be with us. It's very disappointing, Della, it really is.

ADELA: I'm sorry, Mummy, but this marvellous railway service we hear about let me down. Hello Livvie. Come on, now.

[ADELA *and a red-eyed* OLIVIA *embrace.*]

HUGH: Mrs Hindmarsh, I'm sorry I wasn't able to pay my last respects to Captain Hindmarsh. He was a great man, a pioneer. I would have liked to have been there.

IVY: Never mind, Mr Crane. It rained all afternoon. Charles, go and see how many points have fallen, will you?

[CHARLES *hands her a drink and goes out through the doorway.*]

Yes, he was a good man. Bit crotchety towards the end. He was devoted to Adela, but . . . I suppose she couldn't bear to see him bed-ridden. She's always been impatient with invalids. Just like a little girl. What on earth is this monstrosity doing on the table?

ADELA: I told Frances to use it. Gingham's very fashionable. Especially at Government House.

IVY: You're not going to try that old trick on me, are you Della?

ADELA: Apparently not.

OLIVIA: Why did you have to be late? He was your father.

ADELA: I didn't *have* to be late, Livvie. It wasn't my fault.

IVY: If you wanted to be here, Adela, you would have been here.

ADELA: All right. I was late for my father's funeral. Is that a crime? Surely only a ghoul would be early.

IVY: Are you certain your train was late?

ADELA: Go and visit the driver in the Old Men's Home if you don't believe me.

IVY: [*to* HUGH] Adela has a genius for skirting around anything that smacks of responsibility or unpleasantness.

ADELA: I don't think that's fair.

OLIVIA: I think it's true.

[ADELA *turns suddenly and looks around.*]

ADELA: The house looks beautiful, Mummy. You've really kept it up. The only thing I thought of, when I first came in, was this area here, under the staircase.

OLIVIA: Della, you're not going to suggest spending *more* money on the house?

ADELA: It's just that people in Sydney are finding that this dead area can be enhanced by an indoor garden.

IVY: Oh, that's interesting.

ADELA: I mean, what use is this cupboard anyway? It's only full of junk. [*Opening the cupboard*] There's nothing here that couldn't be thrown out or stored in the boatshed. Oh. My hoop. Good God.

> [*She pulls out an old wooden hoop and studies it.*]

OLIVIA: Della, don't be silly. We need that cupboard and there's not enough light there for plants.

IVY: Be quiet, Livvie. The only thing that worries me, Della, is the staircase. Would there be enough support?

ADELA: Oh, of course. We'd leave all the beams as they are. I've seen *countless* staircases with gardens under them. Plants like aspidistras don't need light to grow. All the *best* houses have got them already.

IVY: Come here, darling. [*Hugging* ADELA] I felt almost sad when Livvie and Charles grew up, and of course Monica, but I never felt sad about Adela's growing up because of course she never grew up.

OLIVIA: Oh, Mummy, of course she has. She's thirty-six. She's a widow. She's a . . . an adult.

ADELA: You bet.

IVY: She's a child, a little girl who never grew up.

ADELA: This is all complimentary, I take it, about my looks.

IVY: You see. My point is made.

> [IVY *and* ADELA *laugh.*]

OLIVIA: Oh, I just can't help thinking about Daddy.

> [OLIVIA *sits by the table and cries.* IVY *and* HUGH *pace about.*]

ADELA: [*comforting* OLIVIA] Come on, Livvie. We must look ahead. That's what Daddy did. He was always thinking of the future, of the river, of the Murray Valley, all the other rivers, and boats, and exploring and adventure, and planning cities and towns and *all* that sort of thing.

OLIVIA: Don't talk about Daddy any more.

ADELA: No. You're right. I'm sorry. But let's talk about us. The old firm. Livvie, Della and Monny. We'll terrify the district together. We did it once, we can do it again.

OLIVIA: Monica doesn't want me to go out with her any more.

ADELA: I'll straighten that girl out. She'll think a ton of bricks has dropped on her stupid little head.

OLIVIA: She's only young, you know.

ADELA: So am I, Livvie. And beautiful. I've never been ashamed of that.

[IVY *has been looking out the window.*]

IVY: Oh, thank God, here's Monica.

[MONICA HINDMARSH *comes in the front door.*]

MONICA: Hello, Hugh. Sorry about the delay — we got bogged. Adela. Where have you been?

IVY: A good question. I look forward to finding out where she's been.

ADELA: Hiding under the stairs. How are you?

MONICA: Nice to see you.

[*They embrace briefly.*]

Hugh, have you got a drink?

HUGH: Yes thanks. How was it?

MONICA: Oh, bit of an ordeal. I'm hungry after all that. Frances! Frances!

IVY: [*grimacing*] They ought to swap places.

HUGH: Can I get you a drink?

MONICA: I'd *love* a drink.

[*She sits down.* HUGH *gets a glass from the sideboard.*]

So, Della, you did it again.

ADELA: We've been through all that.

MONICA: I'm paying a tribute to your genius. Am I at the end of a long queue?

ADELA: Well, you're behind me, anyway.

OLIVIA: We've already had the house redesigned.

MONICA: Oh, Livvie, give it a rest.

[HUGH *hands her a drink.*]

Thank you, Hugh. Welcome home, Adela.

ADELA: Yes. It is my home.

[LEO MULCAHY *comes in the front door. His feet are bare.*]

MONICA: Leo! Where are your boots?

LEO: Hello, Adela.

ADELA: Leo. What a lovely surprise.

  [*They shake hands warmly.*]

  You'd better satisfy Monica's curiosity.

LEO: She ought to be thankful, not curious. I was up to my ankles in mud for her sake.

ADELA: Don't expect gratitude. She's never affected by anything.

LEO: And are you so different?

ADELA: I'm making up time in leaps and bounds.

  [FRANCES *comes in.*]

MONICA: Frances, could we have some sandwiches and do we have any old boots of my father's that would fit Mr Mulcahy?

LEO: Forget it, Frances. But I will have a sandwich.

IVY: Frances, where's Charles?

FRANCES: He's out the back, Mrs Hindmarsh.

IVY: Then tell him to come in.

FRANCES: Yes, Mrs Hindmarsh.

  [*During the conversation between* LEO *and* ADELA, FRANCES *goes.* MONICA *goes over to* HUGH, *who puts the hoop over her and draws her towards him for a quick kiss.* MONICA *glances quickly around to see if her mother is watching, but* IVY *is staring out the window.* MONICA *kisses* HUGH *and he removes the hoop. They chat quietly by the staircase.*]

LEO: I'm sorry about your father. The river won't be the same without him.

ADELA: *Wombelano* will be a little on the hollow side, too.

LEO: How long are you down?

ADELA: For good.

LEO: You always sound so definite when you say that.

ADELA: Do you think I'm deluding myself when I say I think I'm needed here?

LEO: Have you ever deluded yourself?

ADELA: Oh, yes. I think so. Oh, yes.

LEO: Well, we need something here, that's for sure.

ADELA: Haven't times been good? I'm not referring to your wife.

LEO: I wasn't either. It's just that the grapes aren't making a fortune for your property or mine and the *Werriwa*'s lost a lot of business to the railways.

ADELA: Yes, but surely if Albury becomes the Federal capital we'll be sitting in the sun?

LEO: That's just a rumour.

ADELA: Even if it doesn't, this will be a big city.

LEO: I won't be alive in two hundred years' time.

ADELA: My father said Albury-Wodonga, Swan Hill and Echuca would be big cities and there'd be all sorts of irrigation and a rich countryside and prosperity for everyone.

LEO: I should have said four hundred years.

ADELA: Oh, Leo, you're not becoming an old stick-in-the-mud, are you?

LEO: I'm a bit down, Adela, that's all. My place is too small to make a go of, and I've been doing a few things around *Wombelano* and taking the odd job on the river.

ADELA: I thought your wife said you weren't ever to go back on the river.

LEO: What she said doesn't matter now.

ADELA: Oh. I see. You're cutting loose.

LEO: I'm really down, that's the truth.

ADELA: Why haven't things gone ahead here?

LEO: The river runs through three small-minded colonies. All of them own railways. None of them will spend any money on the river. The only hope is that when Federation comes next year we'll have a national government that'll build the necessary locks and dams and we'll have year-round traffic with no floods or droughts. But even then I fear we've moved twenty years too late. We were on the verge of something twenty years ago. But now I think we've run down.

ADELA: You must be so disappointed.

LEO: Your father was always double-barrelled about it. He would say if we want to change the face of the world then we must forget about fate. But if he came up against a barrier like a flood or a government or simply a new form of transport he would say 'It was fated to happen' and

sleep very soundly. It's been the second barrel for a while
now. Nothing but stagnation.

ADELA: That's so depressing. I can hardly bear to think of it.
This is supposed to be the *new* world. I think we should
all — you know — what's the word I want? *Do* something.

LEO: And they say your father's dead.

ADELA: What are you suggesting? That I'm a parrot?

LEO: No, Adela. You're definitely an individual, just like
your father. Let's hear about all your progress and
development. How's your new job?

ADELA: I didn't like it, so I resigned. My place is here.

LEO: So you mean it when you say you're back for good.

ADELA: I thought you believed me.

LEO: I didn't think you were serious.

ADELA: That's the point. You never take me seriously.

LEO: Adela, I take you seriously but you must admit you
have occasionally changed your mind.

ADELA: *I've* changed. Can you understand that?

LEO: As long as you'll still be my best mate.

ADELA: I haven't changed that much.

LEO: You have in one respect.

ADELA: What's that?

LEO: You look a bit frightened.

ADELA: Frightened of what?

LEO: Oh, I can't pinpoint that. But you do admit the charge
in general?

ADELA: No, I don't think so.

LEO: No?

ADELA: Perhaps just a little bit, in the evenings. But I'll get
over it.

LEO: All of my best mates do.
    [FRANCES *brings the food in.*]

IVY: At last! Come on, Livvie, have something to eat.
    [IVY *pats* OLIVIA *on the shoulder as they all converge
    on the food.* MONICA *starts towards the table, and*
    HUGH *drops the hoop over her. She laughs and takes
    the hoop off.*]
    Monica!

MONICA: I'm sorry, Mummy.

HUGH: It's my fault, Mrs Hindmarsh. You're all taking it so well, I forgot. Perhaps I could propose a small toast, just for a moment, or perhaps Leo might like to.

LEO: You go ahead, Hugh.

HUGH: Well, let me just say, to a great man, who left a great legacy, and who had great vision. Captain Hindmarsh.

[*They drink.* MONICA *squeezes* HUGH's *hand and then puts her arm around* OLIVIA.]

IVY: Yes. Yes. Thank you, Hugh. Yes, he was a good man.

ADELA: Mummy, I'm sorry. I should have come down yesterday.

IVY: It's all right, darling. We're all here now.

[LEO *takes a couple of sandwiches and sits in the chair by the front door.* ADELA, MONICA, *and* OLIVIA *stay in a huddle by the table.* FRANCES *goes over to the door.*]

FRANCES: The coach is here with your baggage, Mrs Learmonth.

ADELA: Thank you, Frances. I need a volunteer.

[ADELA *looks at* HUGH. HUGH *makes for the door.*]

Thank you, Hugh.

[HUGH *goes out.* FRANCES *goes out, through the doorway.* IVY *takes* LEO *a glass of punch.*]

IVY: You should have helped yourself, Leo.

LEO: I'm off that.

IVY: Really? A leopard changing its spots. Not that you're a leopard, of course. Forgive me. Thank you for coming today. The others were mostly useless. Still, to be fair to them, they're harder hit than you.

LEO: Not by much. I'd still be a river rat if it weren't for your husband. What will you do now?

IVY: I've been trying not to give that any thought.

LEO: Do you want to go?

IVY: Do you think I'm being disloyal when I say I've always wanted to go?

LEO: No . . . I don't.

IVY: Be honest with me.

LEO: Your husband only wanted his family to be happy in what they were doing.

IVY: He said that, but he didn't mean it. It was his way of

letting people down easily. People he knew couldn't
change themselves.

LEO: Then what did he want of you all?

IVY: After forty years I can truthfully say I don't know. I
might have known once, but if I did it's gone. And it
probably went because he was so vague. Now I'm too
tired even to think about it. I'd just as soon move back to
Melbourne and forget all about it.

LEO: Then do that.

IVY: Don't you disapprove?

LEO: It'd be going against my interests.

IVY: Oh?

LEO: I want to be full-time manager of *Wombelano*.

IVY: That's quite a sudden step for you.

LEO: No one knows the place like me. You could retire to
Melbourne or go overseas and know I'd get the maximum
out of it. The maximum for the rest of your days. I'm no
saint, but you know I'm honest and you could only hope
for that with someone else.

IVY: George and I always thought that *Wombelano* would
go to one or more of our children.

LEO: Who?

IVY: Charles.

LEO: There's no future for him here. What have you got?
Twenty acres of vineyards and orchards. The biggest
property in the area is forty acres. Whatever the recently
departed might have thought, this is the place for a small
businessman, someone who'll settle for it. Charles ought
to join the navy or go up north.

IVY: There's also the *Werriwa*.

LEO: That boat's an albatross. The most you can hope for is
the odd excursion party.

IVY: George thought the river was the future.

LEO: You said he was vague.

IVY: Yes. What if Charles insists on staying?

LEO: Ah well. But I think he'll want something more or
something else. Who in your family has it in them to be a
small businessman?

IVY: Apart from me . . .

[*They smile at each other.* LEO *puts the sandwiches in his pocket and starts rolling up his trouser legs.*]

LEO: I'd reported you as missing.

IVY: Oh, and of course Adela. Now there's a fine business brain for you. She couldn't run her money-box at a profit.

LEO: She does have an engaging habit of running out of steam.

IVY: She'll be back at her job on Monday. I'm going to Sydney to visit her soon.

LEO: But she's resigned.

IVY: What?

LEO: She just told me.

[HUGH *comes in the front door. He is carrying a huge trunk.*]

ADELA: Oh. The upstairs landing, thank you Hugh.

[HUGH *sets off, staggering up the stairs.*]

Careful now. (*To* MONICA) He's doing a fine job.

MONICA: I'm so glad.

[IVY *is looking a bit ashen-faced.*]

LEO: Come on, buck up. She'll be good for the place. Prodigal daughters always are.

IVY: Yes, I must try to picture it as a blessing.

LEO: Look, I'd better go, I meant to save all this up for a day or two, but if it's made your job any easier . . .

IVY: Don't worry about me. If there's one thing I am, and it sets me apart from all the dreamers around here, it's practical.

LEO: I'll rely on that. Well, I'll make a dash.

IVY: You could take the coach.

LEO: Not worth the trouble. But I will have one sip. For Captain Hindmarsh.

[*He takes a sip from the glass she has been holding, then looks out the front door.*]

Curse this rain. I'll have to change the mooring of my punt.

IVY: I hear the punt's become your livlihood.

LEO: You can change that. Just don't make me . . .

IVY: Suffer?

LEO: Yes. Let's leave it at that. Goodbye. Goodbye
    everyone.

ADELA: Goodbye, Leo.

    [LEO *goes.* IVY *looks after him.* ADELA *wanders across*
    to join her. HUGH *joins* MONICA.]

    Isn't he nice? He's so . . . I don't know . . . solid. I mean
    he's a presence.

OLIVIA: I don't see how he could be an absence.

ADELA: Oh, Livvie, try not to be boring. You know what I
    mean. Leo's . . . there. You know?

OLIVIA: One time his wife was here. She stole some of our
    silver.

ADELA: No.

IVY: Be fair, Olivia. The woman was mad at the time. If
    anyone's to be criticised it's Mr Mulcahy. He did nothing
    about it.

ADELA: Obviously he was humouring the woman.

OLIVIA: In which case we'd have had the silver returned.

ADELA: I think he's solid and nice, like an old tiger. I feel so
    sorry for him, having to look after that horrible broom-
    stick wife of his.

IVY: Adela!

OLIVIA: Mrs Mulcahy died a few months ago.

ADELA: Oh. I'm sorry. Why wasn't I told?

IVY: I assumed Livvie mentioned it in a letter. Besides, we've
    had other problems.

ADELA: What must he think of me?

MONICA: I don't know why you're so entranced by him.
    Everyone knows he smuggles cattle across the border.

ADELA: Everyone knows because they do it themselves.

HUGH: Anyway, all that border tax business is going to stop
    in the new year.

MONICA: Why should it?

HUGH: Because of Federation. That's why we're federating.

ADELA: Oh, Monny, who would ever accuse Leo of being
    an out-and-out thief?

OLIVIA: Well, what was his father?

ADELA: I don't know. What?

IVY: His father was what they call a true patriot.

[OLIVIA *looks at her inquiringly.*]
He left his country for his country's good.

ADELA: Tell me this: why are you ganging up on poor Leo?

OLIVIA: We're not ganging up on him and it's nothing personal. It's just that before Daddy got sick — not long before — I organised a dinner party for some navy people from Melbourne — they came up for three days and it was wonderful — just like years ago — and on the night of the dinner party — you should have seen the officers — absolutely impeccable, it was such a pleasure and I thought if only things could be . . . not that I've ever been unhappy here, although this past year . . . we've never really made friends around here . . .

[*Pause.*]

MONICA: Mrs Mulcahy came up to sell some vegetables and then she did the evil deed. Leo's been sniffing around a lot — particularly lately — but no sign of the silver.

IVY: Has Leo been sniffing around a lot? I haven't noticed.

MONICA: I think you can be excused for being pre-occupied, Mummy.

IVY: Yes. Yes. I love dear Leo, but I just can't see him in charge of *Wombelano*. He's a lovely man, but it wouldn't be my idea of heaven to find him in the living room at all hours.

[IVY *looks searchingly around the room.*]

MONICA: Surely Leo would never be in charge of *Wombelano*?

IVY: [*staring at the tablecloth*] No . . . he wouldn't. I can't bear this cloth another minute. Frances!

ADELA: I think it looks very smart and appropriate.

OLIVIA: I think it looks ghastly. This is a wake.

[FRANCES *comes in.*]

IVY: Exactly. Go and get one of those new white tablecloths, Frances.

FRANCES: But Mrs Hindmarsh, one's dirty and the other's for the dining room. It'll only cover half of this table.

IVY: Then so be it. Did you tell Charles to come here?

FRANCES: Yes, Mrs Hindmarsh. He's on his way.

[*She goes out quickly.*]

IVY: Gingham. Anyway, it's dirty now.

OLIVIA: Excuse me, everyone.

   [OLIVIA *dashes upstairs.*]

IVY: If only Charles were as conscientious as Olivia.

ADELA: Poor Livvie. She would have been the greatest naval hostess of both of these centuries. The only problem is that Albury, like Switzerland, has no navy. But let's not be pessimistic. I look forward to a bracing regimen of plain meals and reading lots of solid books on the verandah. Plus of course the care and growth of my family.

   [IVY *and* MONICA *exchange glances.* CHARLES *comes in holding an empty rain gauge.*]

CHARLES: I found the rain gauge. There's nothing in it. Someone left it lying on the verandah.

IVY: What on earth took you so long?

CHARLES: I had to look for the gauge.

HUGH: Now that you're here, have a drink with us.

   [HUGH *pours some punch into the gauge.* CHARLES *holds it up.*]

CHARLES: I was going to put this out by the front gate.

HUGH: You can still do it.

   [CHARLES *grins and drains the gauge.*]

IVY: How's the rain, or didn't you notice?

CHARLES: It's slackening off. We'll be all right.

IVY: Well if it sets back in I want everything moved up from the boatshed. Everything. And you're in charge. Do you understand?

CHARLES: Yes.

HUGH: You've never been threatened by floods here, have you?

IVY: Not here in the house, but everywhere else. We were nearly marooned once.

CHARLES: I'll take the gauge out the front.

IVY: Charles, will you sit down, please?

   [CHARLES *hesitates, then sits, fiddling with the gauge.*]
   And please put that stupid thing away.

HUGH: I'll take it out.

   [HUGH *takes the gauge and goes out the front door.*]

IVY: Charles, I've been meaning for some time now — perhaps the greater part of your lifetime — to ask you what precisely it is that you want to do.

ADELA: He wants to go up to his room.

MONICA: Adela . . .

ADELA: I'm not trying to be flippant, Mummy. I'm trying to be sympathetic.

IVY: I had a daughter at Government House. Now she's resigned so that she can be sympathetic.

ADELA: How did you know I've resigned?

IVY: Leo told me.

ADELA: Damn Leo. Mummy, I don't want us to argue. I just want us all to be happy together.

IVY: I was going to visit you . . .

ADELA: I've come here instead. And my first act will be to stop you from bullying poor Charles.

CHARLES: Don't be stupid, Della. I don't need your help.

ADELA: Charles, I was being flippant.

MONICA: Come on, Della. Let's go out on the verandah and see if Hugh's been drowned.

ADELA: No! I want to know why you've asked Charles what he's going to do.

IVY: Because I'm by nature curious and interfering.

ADELA: What's going to happen to *Wombelano*?

IVY: I don't know.

ADELA: You do know.

IVY: Adela, you're not too old to be asked to go to your room.

ADELA: I have never heard of a case, last century or this, of a thirty-six year-old widow being asked to go to her room.

MONICA: I think Mummy wants to discuss this with Charles first.

ADELA: Monica, you are so sensible and level-headed that I'm convinced you were left on the doorstep. Now, Mummy, may I please have an answer?

IVY: I may leave *Wombelano* to Charles...

ADELA: Oh yes, that's perfect. And the rest of us can stay for ever under his benevolent rule.

IVY: ...or I may ask Mr Mulcahy to help out. Or I may

appoint you manager and sack you the following day in
response to public pressure.

ADELA: Let's not even *consider* those *chilling* possibilities.
My vote goes to Charles.

CHARLES: [*turning to* IVY] Are you going to send her to her
room?

ADELA: I'll go. You and Charles must have a lot of details to
work out. Call me if you need me.

> [*She takes* MONICA's *arm and they head for the
> doorway.*]

MONICA: When did I become level-headed?

ADELA: Little Monny!

MONICA: I protest.

> [ADELA *laughs as they leave.* CHARLES *gets himself a
> drink.*]

IVY: I did ask you a question.

CHARLES: Why do there have to be any decisions? Why can't
we carry on? Each of us has a part to play.

IVY: What if you decide to marry instead of fooling around
with town girls?

CHARLES: I'm sure my wife would be welcome here.

IVY: Do you think she would enjoy having two widows and
two spinsters around the place?

CHARLES: Monica surely won't be a spinster for ever.

IVY: It wouldn't work, Charles, and in any case I want to
travel just once more.

CHARLES: Leo Mulchahy wouldn't make a go of it.

IVY: Why not?

CHARLES: He's too small-minded.

IVY: Good. That qualifies him to run *Wombelano*.

CHARLES: But there's more to it than *Wombelano*. There's
the river, there's the *Werriwa*.

IVY: I think we should sell the *Werriwa*.

CHARLES: What? With Father only buried today you want
to --

IVY: You can stop that!

> [IVY *regains her composure.*]

CHARLES: I can run the *Werriwa*. Soon we'll have locks and
dams and canals not just here but all the way to Adelaide

and all the way up the Darling. Do you know there are tropical rainforests in Queensland which could feed pipelines into the Darling? Have you thought what that could mean?

IVY: Charles, the *Werriwa* has become a losing investment.

CHARLES: That's just temporary. I'll make it pay. I know that ship and I know the river and I'll take every kind of product up and down it seven days a week until it pays and then I'll buy another ship. There'll be none of this excursion nonsense. That ship is for passengers and cargo.

IVY: What about *Wombelano*?

CHARLES: I've been effectively running it for the last year. I can handle *Wombelano*.

IVY: You've never thought of doing anything else?

CHARLES: What?

IVY: The navy.

CHARLES: Father preferred it here. I've got no doubt he was right.

IVY: Yes, but he discovered that himself.

CHARLES: Are you suggesting that there's no such thing as accumulated wisdom, that we can't pass knowledge on to others?

IVY: No, Charles. It was just a thought.

CHARLES: Why think something alien?

IVY: Because I'm tired. Because I want you to realise your potential. Because I don't think it would be a bad idea to sell everything here and go and enjoy some city living for a change.

CHARLES: What, sell the whole . . ?

IVY: Yes.

[*Pause.*]

What's the matter?

CHARLES: I'm just trying to imagine what Father would have said.

IVY: That won't help us.

CHARLES: Did you tell him of your plans? Last week, perhaps?

IVY: Oh, Charles, no.

CHARLES: Do you think he would have wanted me to keep things going here?

> [IVY *nods and cries.*]

I think he had enough faith in you to ... I'm sorry, Mother.

IVY: No more, Charles. The day has come to an end for me. I want to go up to my room.

CHARLES: Let me help you.

> [*He helps her up the stairs.* MONICA *comes out on to the verandah and sits in the swing seat.* IVY *stops.*]

IVY: We won't change anything for now.

CHARLES: Good.

> [HUGH *comes on to the verandah in bare feet with his trousers rolled up.*]

MONICA: Hugh, what happened?

HUGH: Let's just say I survived the bog but my boots didn't.

> [HUGH *sits on the seat beside* MONICA. IVY *and* CHARLES *disappear upstairs.*]

MONICA: You poor thing. We've put you to work already.

HUGH: It's the country way.

MONICA: Yes, isn't it? Just consider. Albury must be the most boring, isolated place in the universe. And *Wombelano*'s isolated from Albury.

HUGH: You don't consider the Murray the hub of the civilised world?

MONICA: Do you?

HUGH: It's nice enough to look at, but I can see why they call it 'Sleepy Hollow'. The people are a bit limited.

MONICA: The people are plebs. Except of course for me.

HUGH: You know what I'd like to do with you?

MONICA: Do I want to hear this?

HUGH: I think so.

MONICA: That doesn't sound very definite.

HUGH: You *need* to hear this.

MONICA: Now I do feel frightened. Do you think I should try to escape?

HUGH: I can run faster than you in bare feet.

MONICA: All right. Let me know the worst.

HUGH: I'd like to take you away to Sydney with me.

MONICA: Oh.

HUGH: You're not surprised.

MONICA: I'm trying to seem offended. Can you imagine what the talk would be like in town? Dean Street would be in flames.

HUGH: Not if we were married.

[*Pause.*]

MONICA: That requires a lot of thought.

HUGH: Will you let me know?

MONICA: Yes. I'll let you know.

[*They kiss.* HUGH *breaks off the kiss.*]

HUGH: Wait a minute. You mean you would have come without being married?

MONICA: Certainly not.

[MONICA *resumes the kiss.* FRANCES *comes on and clears the table. She goes out to the kitchen, taking the gingham cloth with her.* ADELA *comes on to the verandah. She is crying.*]

Adela, what's the matter?

ADELA: My father's dead.

MONICA: Well, yes.

ADELA: I've only just realised.

MONICA: Let's try not to dwell on it.

ADELA: Have you thought, Monny, what will we do without him?

[MONICA *and* HUGH *are stumped and saddened by this.* FRANCES *comes on with a fresh white tablecloth, which she flutters out and lays on the table. It covers only about half of the table.* FRANCES *goes out.* ADELA *gazes down at the river. Fade out.*]

END OF ACT ONE

ACT TWO

Spring at Wombelano

October 1900. Morning.

BEN BROMLEY *stands looking at a new garden under the stairs. It has replaced the old cupboard.* BEN *turns and looks at the table. He goes over and samples a grape from a bunch on the table.* IVY *appears at the top of the staircase.*

IVY: Mr Bromley.

BEN: Good morning, Mrs Hindmarsh. Am I disturbing your day?

> [IVY *comes down the stairs.*]

IVY: Not at all. But we are going on a picnic . . .

> [*She stops on the stairs, halfway down.*]

Oh! I've forgotten my hat.

BEN: I'll be brief, Mrs Hindmarsh. Brief, fair, and swift.

> [IVY *hesitates.*]

IVY: Very well. I hope to go part of the way with you.

> [*She comes down the stairs.*]

BEN: I was admiring your garden. It's a clever use of space.

IVY: Yes, that was a dead area.

BEN: I admire the mind that thought it up.

IVY: Yes, there's a lot to be said about that mind.

BEN: Mrs Hindmarsh, as a realtor I must confess my disappointment at the attitude of the smallholders on this bank of the river. I refer to Leo Mulcahy.

IVY: Poor Leo.

BEN: Yes. I made a genuine offer to buy his little place, but he refused. He said he was about to 'turn the corner' in some mysterious way.

IVY: We all have our dreams.

BEN: I know you won't misunderstand me when I say the son of a tyke thief quite often fails to perceive the direction of his true interests.

IVY: Of course not.

BEN: My next stop was *Wombelano* . . .

IVY: Yes?

BEN: I want to buy it outright. I'm sure we can agree on a price.

[*There is a pause while* IVY*'s mind races ahead.*]

It's my aim, Mrs Hindmarsh, to secure all the properties on this bank, to get rid of the vineyards and to run one big orchard. I've decided that apples and pears are the goers and that grapes have had it. Apples and pears are real food, but grapes ... incidentally, what variety are those grapes?

IVY: Wax.

BEN: Oh. Anyway, this'll never be a wine-drinking country.

IVY: Your view of the future is different from my husband's.

BEN: If I am unique, then so be it.

IVY: Who's backing you?

BEN: My realty firm.

IVY: Which is city-based, if I recall?

BEN: Yes.

IVY: London being the city.

BEN: Yes.

IVY: And you are authorised to ...

BEN: That's why I'm here.

IVY: What about the *Werriwa*?

BEN: That wouldn't be my concern. Why don't I call again next week, when you've had time to adapt yourself to the prospect of selling up.

IVY: What if Mr Mulcahy won't sell?

BEN: His holding is not the linchpin of my scheme, Mrs Hindmarsh, and, not to mince words, neither is your little spread. Besides, I expect Mr Mulcahy to be in gaol before the year is out.

IVY: No.

[BEN *goes over to his bag and takes out a branding iron.* MONICA *comes in the front door.*]

MONICA: Hello, Ben. I was down by the river and I saw you come in.

BEN: You're looking beautiful, Monica, and your eyesight must be excellent.

MONICA: It was your purposeful stride that gave you away.

BEN: I enjoyed our meeting at the tennis party.

MONICA: Thank heavens you were there.

BEN: Wasn't the best, was it?

MONICA: Olivia had a great time. What are you threatening my mother with?

[IVY *takes the branding iron from* BEN.]

BEN: Just a branding iron I found by the side of the road. I wondered who owned it.

MONICA: We don't run cattle.

BEN: Some people do. It was just a thought.

IVY: Leo Mulcahy doesn't run cattle either.

BEN: No. But if he should ever take up smuggling cattle across the river then he would face a gaol term of reasonable duration. He would be unable to help you around here and his property would eventually fall to my firm. You would be surrounded by the future, Mrs Hindmarsh.

IVY: You're certainly — in every sense — a speculator, Mr Bromley.

[*He takes back the iron.*]

MONICA: Whom have you come to see?

BEN: I'm very glad to see you . . .

[MONICA *smiles.*]

. . . but I came to see your mother.

MONICA: I bet I know why. And I know you've come to see the wrong person.

BEN: How's that?

MONICA: You want to buy *Wombelano*, is that right?

BEN: Yes.

MONICA: Then you should see Charles, not my mother.

BEN: Charles? But I'm not interested in the boat.

MONICA: Do I have to write it out for you? *Wombelano*'s been left to Charles.

[BEN *looks at* IVY.]

IVY: Monica's right, I suppose, although it's not formal yet.

BEN: Then I have come to see the wrong person. On all counts. Why didn't you tell me?

IVY: She didn't give me a chance.

BEN: Thank you for saving my time, Monica.

MONICA: You're not going, are you? Charles is taking an excursion party out in the *Werriwa*. We're all going, too, for a picnic. Why don't you join us?

BEN: I think I'll pass, thank you.

MONICA: We'd love you to come.

BEN: Thank you, Monica.

MONICA: Then you'll come?

BEN: I've nothing to celebrate.

[CHARLES *comes down the stairs.*]

Congratulations, Charles.

[BEN *goes out the front door.* CHARLES *pauses halfway down the stairs.*]

CHARLES: Why congratulations?

MONICA: He's just heard about your success with the *Werriwa*. Making it pay with all the trippers and tourists.

[CHARLES *smiles and continues down the stairs.*]

CHARLES: It's just work, and work is necessary. Haven't I told you, haven't I lectured you about the joys and responsibilities of hard work and empire-building?

MONICA: It's been days now.

CHARLES: We're slipping, I can feel it.

[MONICA *grins and hugs him.*]

Is everyone ready?

IVY: Not yet. Why don't you go on ahead and warm up.

CHARLES: All right, but don't be late. We've got to pick them up in Albury within the hour.

IVY: I'll crack the whip.

[FRANCES *comes out with* CHARLES' *hat.*]

FRANCES: Excuse me, Mrs Hindmarsh, but I've cleaned the hat.

IVY: Give it to Charles, will you.

[FRANCES *hands the hat to* CHARLES.]

CHARLES: Thank you, Frances. I thought it'd been stolen.

IVY: Frances got the idea. How do you think he looks?

FRANCES: Very handsome, Mrs Hindmarsh.

IVY: Yes, you look very nice, Charles. Thank you, Frances.

[FRANCES *goes.*]

MONCIA: I love that hat. It reeks of authority and power and justice.

CHARLES: [*smiling*] Don't expect too much, Monny.

MONICA: Oh, I will, I will.

[*She kisses him.* HUGH *comes in the front door.*]

CHARLES: Hugh! Thank God. Perhaps you can restrain
    Monica.

HUGH: You have a go. Good morning, Mrs Hindmarsh.

MONICA: What are you doing here, Hugh?

HUGH: You invited me to go for a picnic.

MONICA: Oh, that's right.

HUGH: Is something wrong?

MONICA: No, I just forgot, that's all.

IVY: Monica, is this supposed to be smart behaviour of
    some kind?

MONICA: No, Mummy.

HUGH: Thank you, Mrs Hindmarsh, but I know how moody
    Monica can be.

CHARLES: I'll leave you lot to gather yourselves together.
    Who's bringing the lunch?

IVY and MONICA: Olivia.

    [MONICA *giggles*.]

IVY: Now, Monica. You go on ahead, Charles.

    [ADELA *comes in through the doorway, rolling her
    hoop in front of her. In her other hand she balances a
    small watering can. She wears a long white bathing
    robe.*]

ADELA: Hello, everybody.

    [*She catches the hoop.*]

IVY: What are you doing, Adela?

ADELA: Exercise, Mummy. You should try it.

IVY: I mean in that outfit. You can't come on a picnic
    looking like that.

ADELA: I'm not going on the picnic. I'm going swimming
    instead.

    [*She drops the robe off her shoulders and spins around
    to reveal a swimming costume.*]

IVY: That'll do. I knew you'd find some way of avoiding
    coming with us.

ADELA: I'm not avoiding a family outing. I don't want to be
    swamped by all those dreadful excursion people.

CHARLES: We have to make our peace with them, Della, or
    the ship will run at a loss.

ADELA: *You* make peace and I'll go for a swim. Why don't
    you come with me, Charles? You could get Leo to take

over. You can't work seven days a week.

CHARLES: Thanks, Della, but I have to. If we don't make the place pay, then —

ADELA: Then no one can go swimming. Thank you for the paternal advice.

CHARLES: I've got to relieve the guard. You'll excuse me, Della?

[CHARLES *goes out the front door.* ADELA *leans on the front door, watching him go.*]

HUGH: What did he mean, the guard?

IVY: We've had to guard the *Werriwa* day and night for the last week. Someone tried to cut it loose.

HUGH: Why?

IVY: I should imagine competition had something to do with it.

HUGH: Who do you think would —

IVY: You can discuss that sort of thing with Charles.

MONICA: Mummy, I think I'll stay home.

IVY: Monica, if you dare follow Adela's example . . .

HUGH: We'll have a good time.

IVY: You're coming with us, do you understand?

MONICA: [*sulkily*] Yes.

[OLIVIA *comes in from the kitchen carrying a hamper.*]

OLIVIA: Oh, you're all here.

IVY: Yes, Livvie.

OLIVIA: I've got sandwiches — chicken and beef — and some wine and tea — it's made up so we don't have to use any of that dirty hot water from the boat — and fruit and do we need some raisins? No? No?.

IVY: Don't worry about raisins.

OLIVIA: How many are there again? Let's see. One, two —

ADELA: Have you got tea?

OLIVIA: Yes, and it's already made up.

[MONICA *giggles.*]

What's Monica doing? Oh . . . didn't I already tell you that . . . ? No? No?

ADELA: Yes, Livvie.

OLIVIA: Oh, I see. [*Forcing a laugh*] You think I'm fussing . . . yes . . . now, what was I . . . oh yes, how many of us are there? One, two —

ADELA: I'm not going.

OLIVIA: Not going on the picnic?

ADELA: That's right.

OLIVIA: But I thought you were.

IVY: For God's sake, Livvie, let's go.

OLIVIA: Just a minute, Mummy, I want to check that we've got enough. Monica, stand still, will you?

[MONICA *and* ADELA *assume motionless positions.*]

OLIVIA: Now we've got twenty-four sandwiches and eight mugs.

MONICA: You said you were going to count us.

OLIVIA: Oh what are you doing, Monica? Are you trying to confuse me?

ADELA: Livvie, you're in one of your states. Now just calm down.

OLIVIA: I'm not in a state, no thanks to you.

ADELA: Good. Carry on.

OLIVIA: Now let's see. One, two —

IVY: My hat! I meant to get it when that Bromley was here. I won't be a minute.

[IVY *goes upstairs.*]

OLIVIA: Who's Bromley?

HUGH: Let's make a start.

ADELA: Just a minute, Hugh. Was Ben Bromley here?

MONICA: Yes. He made a bid for *Wombelano*. Unsuccessfully.

ADELA: What did Charles say?

MONICA: He wasn't here. Mummy handled it.

ADELA: That old schemer. When is she *finally* going to hand it over to Charles?

OLIVIA: Are you calling Mummy an old schemer?

MONICA: Yes, it's a bit unfair, Della. Bromley walked out the door with nothing.

ADELA: If I sense something, it's worth a thousand facts. How often have I proved that?

OLIVIA: I don't know.

ADELA: Neither do I, Livvie, but let's pretend I'm right, because the issue is greater than the person.

MONICA: What issue?

ADELA: Can't you see what's happening around you? In her

heart, Mummy wants to sell *Wombelano*. She's weakening daily. Now think what that would mean. Our father wanted Charles to inherit everything, and that's how it should be. There'll always be a home for us here. For you, Livvie, the greatest hostess and organiser in the Riverina. A loyal daughter and affectionate sister. What would you do otherwise? Where would you go?

OLIVIA: I suppose I'd move back to Melbourne with Mummy.

ADELA: Oh, Livvie, what kind of fate is that? Looking after an old invalid and checking through the grocer's bills. What would you do on a Sunday afternoon?

OLIVIA: [*rummaging through the hamper*] I'm sure I've got enough food. I won't bother to count everyone, because not everyone's here.

ADELA: You'll rot in Melbourne, Livvie, and your life won't mean a thing. But here, you're part of the place.

OLIVIA: Stop it, Della. Please.

ADELA: Livvie, those people you romance about — naval officers and all that whirl — do you think, realistically, that you and Mummy will be welcomed as the new society lions? Do you think that?

[OLIVIA *turns away.* MONICA *goes to her.*]

MONICA: Honestly, Della. Is this meant to be helpful?

ADELA: Is she upset? I mean, really upset?

MONICA: Of course she's upset. She was in a state to begin with.

ADELA: Oh, Livvie, I'm sorry. I didn't mean to speak harshly. Now you be careful or you'll set me off, too.

OLIVIA: I'm all right. Really. I'm fine.

ADELA: Oh, you have set me off.

[*She wipes her eyes.*]

HUGH: We know you didn't mean it.

[ADELA *pats* HUGH's *arm.*]

ADELA: Thank you, Hugh. [*To* OLIVIA] I didn't intend anything malicious. I just wanted with all my heart to warn you. And you too, Monny. We must put everything we have behind Charles. He must be allowed to run *Wombelano* and we must help him with the *Werriwa*.

He's got so many problems and we must help, help, help.

MONICA: It's all right for you to say. How long have you been part of the place?

[ADELA *gathers herself.*]

ADELA: Hugh. Let me appeal to your objectivity. Should we be more concerned with recriminations or with unity?

HUGH: You put your case very objectively.

ADELA: [*looking at* HUGH *with sudden coldness*] You and Monica just want to cut and run, don't you?

HUGH: Now you are being malicious.

MONICA: And you're a step ahead of me.

ADELA: Oh?

MONICA: I haven't decided whether I want to —

ADELA: Oh, you've never known what you want!

HUGH: I can't agree with that.

[IVY, *wearing her hat, appears at the top of the stairs. She starts to come down.*]

MONICA: Oh, thank God, here's Mummy.

IVY: Are we all finally ready?

HUGH: Nothing can stop us now, Mrs Hindmarsh.

IVY: Good. Enjoy your swim, Adela.

[OLIVIA *hugs* IVY *and runs out the front door.*]

Well! She *is* in a state. Come on, you two.

[IVY *goes out with* HUGH *and* MONICA. ADELA *watches them go and then wanders over and picks up her watering can. She waters the garden under the stairs.* FRANCES *carries some freshly ironed sheets in and starts up the stairs.* ADELA *hurls the watering can at the floor.* FRANCES *stops halfway up the stairs.*]

FRANCES: What's going on?

ADELA: Nothing, Frances. I'm just a disappointed swimmer.

FRANCES: A what?

ADELA: You carry on.

[ADELA *picks up the watering can.* FRANCES *hesitates, then continues up the stairs.*]

Frances, are you happy here?

FRANCES: I think so, miss.

ADELA: I think I am, too. But I suppose it's a bit early for a verdict.

FRANCES: Yes, miss.

> [*She starts back up the stairs. She is nearly at the top when suddenly* EVAN LEE *and* LEO *burst in the front door propping up* CHARLES, *whose trouser legs are bloody and torn.* FRANCES *drops the sheets all over the place and screams.*]

ADELA: Charles! What happened? My God, your legs are — Evan! It's you!

EVAN: Yes, Adela. Now stand back, please.

CHARLES: I'm all right, I'm all right.

LEO: There was a fire in the engine room.

> [*They set him down on a chair and recover their breath.* OLIVIA *runs in.*]

OLIVIA: What can I do, tell me what can I do?

EVAN: Get the kitchen ready. Bandages, everything. Quick!

FRANCES: I'll do it, Dr Lee.

> [*She rushes out.*]

EVAN: Go and help her!

OLIVIA: Oh . . . yes.

> [OLIVIA *rushes out, dropping the hamper.*]

LEO: The glass on the temperature gauge exploded and went everywhere.

ADELA: Thank god his face is unmarked.

LEO: He must have turned his back on it and then fallen on his stomach.

CHARLES: This is ridiculous. I've got to go. I'll lose the excursion. Don't you idiots realise that? I've got a living to make.

> [*He tries to get up, but* LEO *restrains him.*]

LEO: Come on, Charles. That's it for today.

> [IVY *bursts in, holding* CHARLES' *hat and jacket.*]

IVY: Hugh and Monica are bringing the coach around.

EVAN: Good. But I'll have to clean and dress the cuts first.

IVY: Oh Charles, Charles . . .

CHARLES: I'm not hurt. I'm perfectly able to walk. I want to find that bastard.

LEO: Apparently the guard wasn't on the job when Charles got there.

CHARLES: Somone paid him. I'll find them both.

EVAN: Never mind that now. Take his leg.

    [ADELA *grabs* LEO's *arm.*]

ADELA: Leo! Could you take the boat out?

LEO: What a time to think of that!

ADELA: It would calm Charles down, don't you see, if he knew we wouldn't miss out.

LEO: I can't take the boat out. It's damaged.

CHARLES: No . . . no . . . we got to the fire in time.

ADELA: Leo, please.

LEO: No! You'll have to forget it.

CHARLES: I can take it!

    [LEO *and* EVAN *are holding him down.*]

EVAN: Charles, you're finished for the day, and at least for a week. Now shut up and keep still. Right, let's move him.

ADELA: Leo, why won't you —

EVAN: Have you got him?

LEO: Yes.

    [LEO *and* EVAN *carry* CHARLES *through to the kitchen.* BEN *has come in the front door.*]

BEN: Mrs Hindmarsh, please accept my sympathy. If there's anything I can do, just tell me.

ADELA: What are you doing here?

IVY: Adela!

BEN: I went down to Mulcahy's place to have another crack at him, but he was loading his punt and talking business with Dr Lee. Then they started running towards the *Werriwa* and I saw them carry Charles up the hill. It's a terrible business.

ADELA: Dr Lee seems to have it under control.

IVY: What is it, Mr Bromley?

BEN: There was something I forgot to tell you this morning, although it's hardly the time now, I realise. My firm makes loans and gives financial advice to those on the land, such as yourself. I wondered if you'd like to avail yourself of our service, regardless of any other decisions.

ADELA: No thanks.

    [HUGH *and* MONICA *burst in the front door.*]

HUGH: We brought the coach around.

MONICA: Where is he?

IVY: In the kitchen. Wait till Dr Lee says he has to be taken to hospital.

  [MONICA *rushes into the kitchen.*]

BEN: I'd better go.

IVY: No. wait, Mr Bromley. I want to talk to you. Come through here, to the living room.

BEN: You're sure this is the right —

IVY: Yes, yes, yes. Come on.

ADELA: Mummy, we've never been in debt before.

IVY: How would you know?

  [IVY *leads* BEN *out.*]

ADELA: There you have it. They make all the decisions behind my back and then say 'Where were you when we needed you?' Who was that liar who wrote the Prodigal Son? Not one of your stories, was it?

HUGH: It's in the Bible.

ADELA: Of course. You're a modern writer. You're young, contemporary, all of that, and in addition you look frightened.

HUGH: I'm not frightened. Who do you think you're dealing with? A child?

ADELA: I'm sorry. I didn't mean to impugn your vast reserves of courage and tenacity, but you do look a little shaky.

HUGH: I may be a bit shocked, which is understandable.

ADELA: Of course.

HUGH: That's a terrible thing to happen to Charles. Who could have done it? Was it sabotage?

ADELA: Probably. Every so often there's a mysterious fire on board a Murray boat. Sometimes they sink unexpectedly. You know how it was first charted? Two boats had a race for a prize. But apparently now the prize is just to stay afloat. Sometimes I pray for people to take up drinking wine on a big scale.

HUGH: How could that help?

ADELA: We'd get a higher price for our grapes and we wouldn't have to rely on this treacherous river for part of our living.

HUGH: Treacherous is the word. And violent.

ADELA: Not quite the cosy little nest egg one could be led to expect.

HUGH: No . . . it isn't.

ADELA: Perhaps I've exaggerated. I still love the river and I always come back.

[*She looks down at the river.*]

HUGH: You might have been branded or scarred by it, but I can assure you there's not enough here to keep me.

[ADELA *picks up her hoop.*]

ADELA: You're probably right. When I was young I went down to the river one day with just my hoop for company and I walked along the bank until I came to the willows and there was a half-open cavern with a floor of sticks and moss, and it sloped down and then fell away from the rounded walls into the river, which seemed to be neither flowing nor stagnant. I was rather puzzled by this, so I tossed a branch of dead leaves into the river. They floated of course but what threw me was that they didn't move. The river had stopped.

HUGH: It was probably a backwater.

ADELA: Oh, no. With my throwing arm and the small width after a drought, I landed those leaves right in the middle of the river. Then I stood very still. As still as the river.

HUGH: That's where you and I are different. I see no wonder at all in this backwater.

ADELA: No one should think that, but I suppose most people do. My father kept saying, '*This* is the place. *This* is what's important'. But very few agreed with him.

HUGH: I can't wait to get out of here.

[ADELA *considers him.*]

ADELA: With Monica?

HUGH: Her decision won't affect me.

ADELA: Sometimes I wonder how close you are to her.

HUGH: She keeps me wondering that, too.

ADELA: Not intentionally, surely?

HUGH: With every fibre of her being. All I get is that cold little smile.

ADELA: That *is* a problem. Let me think what I can do.

HUGH: Hit her on the head, perhaps.

ADELA: That wouldn't be part of my life's work, which is, as you've gathered by now, to do with care and growth.

HUGH: Oh yes. Does this mean you're going to help us?

ADELA: Yes, I'm afraid it does. Are you going to be a willing patient?

HUGH: I think so.

ADLEA: You won't be put off by my inexperience in the field?

HUGH: It could be an advantage.

ADELA: Good.

[*She kisses him. He gapes at her.*]

HUGH: Why did you do that?

ADELA: To gain your attention.

HUGH: My what?

ADELA: A small failure. But. Nevertheless. A plan is beginning to form in my mind. I won't deny that it's cloudy and I won't be questioned on details but I will tell you this. You are involved.

HUGH: You've got my attention.

ADELA: That was part one of the plan, which is to do with the running of *Wombelano*. I've been worried about the burden on Charles and I think he should share it with others. But who? Olivia is clearly not a leader.

Indispensable on a picnic — yes. And let's not gloss over her unfailing generosity of mind and spirit. But she is not, I feel, a candidate.

HUGH: What about you?

ADELA: I'm the referee.

HUGH: In some ways that's a pity. I'd like you to be available.

ADELA: Now you be careful. I've been known to respond to that sort of thing.

HUGH: I'd like to see you respond.

[*He kisses her. She slowly breaks away.*]

ADELA: We must be objective about this and realise that experience has persuaded me that in any partnership I enter the strength must be provided by the other side.

HUGH: Are you saying I'm weak?

ADELA: Not weak. Unproven. And I'm too old for the unproven.

HUGH: What if I suddenly left the ranks of the unproven?

ADELA: I'm flattered, but I must concentrate on the issues of the day.

HUGH: You want to return to your plan.

ADELA: Yes. My plan.

HUGH: I'm waiting to hear it.

ADELA: Perhaps you won't like the part that involves you.

HUGH: That's possible.

ADELA: *Fixing Up the World*, by Adela Learmonth.

   [*Before* ADELA *can get any further,* EVAN *comes out of the kitchen.*]

   Evan! How is he?

EVAN: All right so far. I got all the glass out of his legs and the girls are tying up the bandages now.

HUGH: I've got the coach here if you want to take him to hospital.

EVAN: We'll see. I've got to get the glass out of his back next.

   [*He offers* ADELA *a cigarette and takes one himself. She gets out her holder. He lights their cigarettes.* HUGH *and* ADELA *exchange glances.*]

   What a job.

HUGH: We're lucky you were so close by.

EVAN: Nothing to it. You don't need a doctor for much. Anyone with good eyes can pick up glass in a pair of tweezers. Still, I'm glad to help out.

ADELA: Thank you, Evan.

EVAN: You hear that? She thanked me. Sitting there in what looks like a towel, smoking like a train, she says in her plummy voice 'Thank you, Evan'. What was the last thing I heard from her? I should remember something vital like that.

ADELA: Evan, not now.

EVAN: That was it. What's this? A carrot patch?

   [*He picks a leaf from the garden under the stairs.*]

ADELA: It's an indoor garden. Haven't you seen them in city houses?

EVAN: No, I'm a country doctor, till I get rich. I suppose it was your idea.

ADELA: Yes. One picks up ideas when one is running other people's households.

EVAN: What have we got here?

[*He crushes the leaf and smells it.*]

Pennyroyal? Mexican cactus? Bound to be something the society ladies have told you to plant.

ADELA: [*to* HUGH] I've always been too conventional for Evan's taste.

EVAN: Adela Learmonth, eh?

ADELA: Yes.

EVAN: How did it happen? I know your father blew up and said he was betrayed, but I never heard your version.

ADELA: I married a doctor, but he was a good deal older. He died of blood poisoning four weeks later.

EVAN: You must have been hit fairly hard.

ADELA: Let's not go into those horrible draughty corridors. It was some time ago.

EVAN: Like us.

ADELA: Oh, no. We were prehistoric. Evan and I used to be partners. That was when he was a bohemian medical student and I was a non-bohemian — at least, to Evan — governess to a fairly large and conventional society family.

EVAN: What a pity you never took the plunge out of there.

ADELA: I think it was just as well for you that I didn't.

EVAN: You hear that? She passed up the opportunity to make a good man out of a complete bastard. I remember what she said: 'There is no place in my life for you.' Isn't that grand? It's a wonder I didn't go for a long swim. Who is this anyway? I didn't catch your name outside.

ADELA: This is Mr Crane.

HUGH: Hugh.

EVAN: Friend of yours?

ADELA: A future relative.

EVAN: Oh. That'll be nice. Any future relatives of Adela's have always been welcome around here. Only thing missing is the old skipper to set you a written and oral examination and then pronounce you unfit to consort with his lovely daughter.

[EVAN *pulls a sandwich out of the hamper and bites into it.*]

ADELA: That never happened.

EVAN: No? Ah well, it won't apply to you now that — with respect — the Captain has left the bridge.

ADELA: I don't think you understand. Hugh's going to marry Monica and live here and help run the place.

EVAN: Oh really? He looks a bit young and a bit surprised to handle all that.

ADELA: He's not surprised. Are you, Hugh?

HUGH: Not any more.

EVAN: And here I was, pairing him off with the wrong sister. Still, they've always been a close family.

ADELA: Do you always have to be vulgar?

EVAN: Listen to that. Vulgar. Now I can hear her mother's voice. Tell me, uh . . .

ADELA: Hugh.

EVAN: Did you have any say in this? I don't mean as far as the choice of sister went — not that they'd try to stick you with Olivia — but as far as choosing any of the sisters went?

ADELA: Of course he did.

EVAN: What are you up to, Adela? Your father's barely cold, your brother's in pain, and here you are, plotting away. We'll have to call you the Black Widow.

HUGH: How is Charles exactly?

EVAN: His legs are fine. We'll see about his back in a minute.

ADELA: Hadn't you better go and see to him?

EVAN: Why don't you?

ADELA: I'm not needed.

EVAN: She doesn't go much on blood. Never has.

ADELA: Will you please go and see to Charles?

EVAN: They'll call me when he's ready.

HUGH: Will he recover completely?

EVAN: We'll see.

ADELA: What do you mean?

EVAN: I don't make predictions. It's a legacy of my time with you. In the meantime, congratulations on your engagement.

HUGH: I'm not engaged.

EVAN: I thought Adela had just given me a detailed

description of your future.

HUGH: Adela's a bit confused and upset.

EVAN: I imagine Monica would be, too, if she knew.

HUGH: Monica doesn't know anything about this.

EVAN: Will she ever get to hear of your plans? Or will they stay locked in Adela's vibrant and wayward little mind?

[HUGH *looks at* ADELA.]

ADELA: She'll get to hear.

[HUGH *moves away from them.* FRANCES *comes in from the kitchen.*]

FRANCES: We're ready for you now, Dr Lee.

EVAN: Good. Never was a nurse more welcome. If you two schemers will excuse me —

[OLIVIA *bustles in.*]

What is it, Olivia?

OLIVIA: We'll need an anaesthetic of some kind.

EVAN: What do you mean?

OLIVIA: We just turned him over, and the glass is pretty deep. I think if we could get him to the hospital . . .

EVAN: I don't really like the idea of moving him yet. Not for a long trip at any rate. We can get all the glass out here and then we'll see. I don't think there's anything to worry about.

OLIVIA: I just know he's going to be in great pain. I can see him feeling towards it in his eyes. He says he's fine and he wants to get up and go, but I can tell it's hurting him and I wish there was something, some kind of anaesthetic we could use to help him. I know I'm not a doctor, but I know he's been hurt and all I can think of is that we must try to soften it in some way.

EVAN: Don't worry, Olivia. You're setting a wonderful example. This girl is the best assistant I've ever had. Cool, efficient, humane, alert — Olivia is without qualification a gem.

ADELA: She's brilliant, there's no doubt. Now will you please go and see to Charles?

EVAN: Come where you're appreciated, Olivia, and you'll see how quickly we can fix him up.

[*He leads her towards the doorway.* FRANCES *steps back suddenly.* CHARLES *walks in, a little jerkily.*]

CHARLES: Hello. Is everyone ready?

OLIVIA: Charles! What are you doing walking around on your legs?

CHARLES: Best means of locomotion yet devised, I'd say.

[LEO *and* MONICA *come in.*]

LEO: Charles! Come back here.

CHARLES: I'm fine. Really. Thank you for your concern. I've suffered a minor flesh wound, that's all.

MONICA: It's not minor.

CHARLES: Yes it is. And the boat, the boat is fine. We're not going to lose the excursion. We can't afford it. Can we, Della? So let's all go down to the boat. We're well prepared for the day. Monica looks ravishing. Hugh looks . . . well, ravished. He's certainly pale. Adela's turned her nose up at the whole thing, but we can accommodate that. Olivia's packed what I'm sure is a beautiful lunch . . .

[*He tries to pick up the hamper, but falters and leaves it on the floor.*]

. . . and she'll bring it down to the *Werriwa*. I think we should all appreciate what we have. A spring day, the vine leaves are as big as dinner plates, a reasonably white boat that may be minus a pressure gauge, but who can tell that when it's out on the river?

[*He has picked his way over to the front door.*]

In fact, I think we should all go. Evan, you must come with us. Now that my father's dead you've no excuse for running out. And Leo, come and have a good time. You've lost your smile. And Frances...Frances too. Why not? Let's all go out on the river and forget that last twenty years. We don't have to remember a thing . . . if we could have one day . . . one spring day together . . . on the river . . .

[*He sways as he goes out the door.*]

EVAN: Someone's certainly gone to work on him.

ADELA: Bring him back, Leo.

MONICA: Please, Leo. He's in a daze.

LEO: You've all made your choice.

[CHARLES *collapses on the verandah.* EVAN *and* HUGH *go out to him.*]

EVAN: Olivia.

OLIVIA: Come on, Frances.

> [OLIVIA *and* FRANCES *go out to the kitchen.*]

MONICA: Why didn't anybody stop him?

> [EVAN *and* HUGH *carry* CHARLES *through to the kitchen.* MONICA *follows them.*]

ADELA: I've never seen him look so driven.

LEO: He's had a lot of pressure put on him.

ADELA: By whom?

LEO: Not you. Not directly.

ADELA: Who, then?

LEO: I don't know. It's not my affair.

ADELA: You could help him. You know this river better than anyone.

LEO: It's not my boat.

ADELA: You want to go now, don't you?

LEO: I was working when this happened.

ADELA: With Evan, I understand.

LEO: Yes. We were loading my punt.

ADELA: Don't tell me Evan's mixed up in this border swindle?

LEO: It's not a swindle. Everyone breaks that stupid law. They're charging thirty shillings now for each head of cattle that goes over the bridge. It's a disgrace.

ADELA: I think the whole business is sordid.

LEO: You can afford to think that.

ADELA: Leo, don't let's quarrel. I've hardly seen you lately. It's been so difficult, trying to build and survive and rescue everything without having you, who know how to get along better than any of us, turn on me and leave me alone.

LEO: It's not like that at all.

ADELA: Then how is it?

LEO: If you can't make a go of *Wombelano*, then sell it. That's the beginning and the end of my one-barrelled advice.

> [*Pause.*]

I've got to go.

ADELA: Goodbye, Leo.

[LEO *starts to go.*]

Thank you for helping Charles. Carrying him up from the
ship, I mean.

[LEO *goes.* MONICA *comes on to the verandah and sinks
down into the swing seat.* ADELA *sits by the table and
wipes blood off her legs.* BEN *comes through the
doorway.*]

BEN: How is Charles?

ADELA: He's fine. Just a few scratches.

BEN: No picnic today, then?

ADELA: Not today.

BEN: What a pity. Well, goodbye.

[*He goes out the front door.* HUGH *joins* MONICA *on the
verandah. She stands up and they kiss passionately.*]

HUGH: Can we go somewhere?

MONICA: Not here.

HUGH: The boat, then. It's empty.

MONICA: Not the boat.

HUGH: Where else?

MONICA: All right. You know that question you asked me?

HUGH: Which one?

MONICA: The big question.

HUGH: Oh, yes.

MONICA: Are you ready for the answer?

HUGH: Yes.

MONICA: It's yes.

[*She kisses him.*]

HUGH: Let's go.

[*They run out.* FRANCES *comes slowly out of the
kitchen into the doorway. She takes out a handkerchief
and shakes it out. She sags against the wall and buries
her face in the handkerchief.*]

ADELA: Frances! What's wrong?

[EVAN *appears in the doorway.*]

Don't tell me.

[*Fade out.*]

END OF ACT TWO

ACT THREE

Federation Ball

December 31, 1900. Evening.

FRANCES *stands on the table, tying balloons onto the chandeliers. There are flowers on the table. A desultory storm can be heard outside. The front door is pushed open and* CHARLES, *who is now confined to a wheelchair, is pushed in by* OLIVIA.

OLIVIA: Look at that rain! On and off all day long. Frances! Help me with Charles' boots, will you?
    [FRANCES *jumps down.*]
FRANCES: Sorry, miss. Got to help with the drinks now.
    [FRANCES *goes out quickly.*]
OLIVIA: That stupid girl. I'm going to speak to Mummy about her. I think she ought to be paid off.
CHARLES: She's given her notice.
OLIVIA: Has she? How do you know?
CHARLES: I've got time to follow all the gossip.
OLIVIA: Well, I'm pleased she's going. Ever since your accident she's been in a flap. She runs as soon as she sees us coming. I don't know why — I'm happy enough to push you around. Now let's see about those boots.
CHARLES: I didn't get wet, really.
OLIVIA: You sure?
CHARLES: Yes, Livvie. And now it's stopped raining.
OLIVIA: [*looking out of the window*] So it has. I'll read you a story, then. We've still got some more of those ones by Washington Irving up our sleeve.
CHARLES: I'd love you to, but don't you want to help get things ready for the ball?
OLIVIA: I've been banned from the kitchen area for unspecified reasons.
CHARLES: Then you should march in there now and straighten them all out.
OLIVIA: Oh no, I'm happy enough. But I will have to get ready soon.

52

CHARLES: You do that, and I'll go to the library with
    Washington Irving.

OLIVIA: Don't you want to meet the guests?

CHARLES: No. It's not as if they're the cream of the land.

OLIVIA: All right. But later on you must come out and see
    the fireworks and drink a toast with us to . . . what?

CHARLES: The new year, the new century, and the new
    country.

OLIVIA: I keep forgetting all that.
    [*What appears to be a tall headless man bursts in the
    front door. It is* BEN.]

BEN: Doctor Lee! Come quick! Doctor Lee! Oh God!
    [OLIVIA *screams.* BEN *takes off his coat, revealing a
    wooden harness built up on his shoulders.*]
    It's only me, Olivia. Sorry about that.

CHARLES: What the hell are you doing?
    [EVAN *comes in quickly through the doorway.*]

BEN: Sorry, Charles. Just playing a trick on Evan. I thought
    I saw him come in here, but he must have come in the
    back way.

EVAN: What are you doing to poor Olivia?

BEN: It was just a joke. There's a party on the bridge
    tonight, and under. For Federation. At midnight the
    Wodonga lot are meeting us in the middle. I had a few
    drinks. None of the townees are at home tonight. They're
    all in the streets, in one big rabble. I'm sorry, Olivia.

OLIVIA: I think you'd better go. Immediately.

BEN: Actually, your mother invited me. I said I'd pop in.
    Should be a good party.

OLIVIA: It's a ball.

BEN: That's right. Many coming?

OLIVIA: No.

EVAN: How are you feeling, Charles?

CHARLES: I'm fine.

EVAN: Good.

BEN: He's adjusted very well.

EVAN: Well, I must say you haven't. You're a bloody
    disgrace.
    [BEN *laughs.*]

CHARLES: Excuse me. I was on my way to the library.

BEN: Why don't you have a drink with us, Charles?

CHARLES: No thanks.

BEN: Come on. Won't hurt you.

OLIVIA: You'll excuse us.

    [OLIVIA *wheels* CHARLES *out.*]

EVAN: That was a fine performance. You ought to try getting a piece of glass wedged into your spine.

BEN: Ah, come on. It was unfortunate and all that, but she made a bit of a meal of it. These Hindmarshes have got to eat a bit of dirt before they die. It's only Mulcahy who's holding them together.

EVAN: You don't have to accept their hospitality.

BEN: What, you think I'm going to hang around with the townees? Besides, I want to put a stop to Mulcahy.

EVAN: What for?

BEN: The man's a criminal.

EVAN: Everyone smuggles across the border. And in any case it'll be legal after midnight. Haven't you heard the news? A nation has been born.

BEN: Mulcahy's not a smuggler. He's a thief. He takes advantage of the fact that everyone turns a blind eye to cattle crossing the river at night.

EVAN: It's all over now, anyway.

BEN: Some of my clients' cattle is still missing.

EVAN: You can't actually *prove* anything against Mulcahy.

BEN: Maybe I can. Maybe not. But at the very least I can bluff him and embarrass him in front of his beloved Hindmarshes. They'll love it. I can look as if I'm going to lay charges against him and then settle for a price — and a good one — for his property.

EVAN: What a way to spend New Year's Eve. Why don't you leave the bodies in the grave?

BEN: What, go easy on Mulcahy?

EVAN: On everybody.

BEN: I tell you straight. I hate that bastard. He ought to be working in a brewery in the city and stealing out of the petty cash box.

EVAN: Why don't I talk to him? You say you'll give him a

good price. Perhaps he'll sell with good grace. Perhaps
he's been put off by your manner, which many keen
judges have at times called abrasive.

BEN: Then he's no businessman.

EVAN: I don't think Leo's ever been accused of being a
tycoon.

BEN: Why are you sticking up for him?

EVAN: That's the first time I've been accused of sticking up
for anyone.

[IVY *and* MONICA *come in through the doorway
followed by* FRANCES, *who carries a bowl of punch.*]

IVY: Mr Bromley. And Evan. Happy New Year and happy
Federation and happy everything. Would you like a
drink?

[FRANCES *puts the bowl on the table.*]

EVAN: I would indeed.

[EVAN *helps himself.*]

IVY: [*to* FRANCES] Take one in to Charles.

FRANCES: Oh.

IVY: Quickly.

[FRANCES *fills a glass and goes.*]

BEN: Hello, Monica.

MONICA: Hello.

BEN: Where have you been hiding?

MONICA: I've been very busy.

BEN: So have I. We must catch up.

MONICA: Catch up on what?

IVY: Monica has been magnificent lately. And Leo's been
teaching Hugh all about the *Werriwa*. Even Adela's been
doing what she can. I'm proud of them all.

BEN: That's good to hear. Why is Leo teaching Hugh about
the *Werriwa*?

IVY: Someone's got to run it. Here, have some punch.

[*She hands him a drink.*]

BEN: Leo's been doing the right thing, has he?

IVY: He's been marvellous. They've all been marvellous.

BEN: Nothing like a bit of adversity to make people
marvellous.

IVY: Adversity? What adversity?

BEN: Charles.

IVY: Oh. Yes.

BEN: That offer of mine. It won't stand for ever, you know.

IVY: I realise that.

BEN: Perhaps tonight isn't the ideal time to ask for a decision.

IVY: No, perhaps not.

BEN: But soon I must know.

IVY: You know, I think I will be able to answer you tonight, Mr Bromley.

BEN: That's marvellous.

IVY: Yes. I can't tell you how proud I am of them all.

BEN: Olivia's obviously doing a very worthwhile job.

IVY: Olivia?

BEN: Looking after Charles.

IVY: Oh. Yes. How are you two getting on?

[*She turns to* EVAN *and* MONICA.]

EVAN: Something must be up. She only promised me one dance.

IVY: Oh, I think something is up, Evan. You'll have to dance with Adela.

EVAN: But I just told Monica it was her or the punch for me tonight.

IVY: At least I can promise you we won't run out of punch. The grapes are from our own vines. Oh, come on, Mr Bromley, stop scowling. Happy New Year.

BEN: You can call me Ben.

IVY: I wouldn't dream of it. Now come on, drink up.

EVAN: Don't say that. He's a nasty drunk and he's already been to one party tonight.

BEN: Where?

EVAN: On the bridge.

BEN: I passed by that on my way to the pub, but I didn't stop.

EVAN: You horrible man. Where's your pride in your community?

BEN: I managed to hide it.

[MONICA *is looking out of the window.*]

IVY: He'll be all right, Monica. I think the girl's in love.

EVAN: She looks worried about something. Hey! Monica! I'm over here.

[*There is no response from* MONICA.]

And they wonder why there are so many drunkards in the Riverina.

[*He refills his glass.*]

IVY: I don't think she'd be upset if you danced with Adela.

EVAN: Thanks for the compliment, but I don't want to hurt anyone's feelings.

IVY: Whose feelings?

EVAN: Adela's. Happy New Year, Ben.

BEN: You're going to leave the place to Hugh and Monica, aren't you?

IVY: Now don't you jump ahead of me, Ben.

EVAN: There's a watershed. She called you Ben.

BEN: I'm getting a bit sick of you.

EVAN: First Monica, now you. I'm a broken man. Will you dance with me, Mrs Hindmarsh?

IVY: As long as you don't call me Ivy.

EVAN: I'll be so well behaved you'll think you're kissing a stranger.

IVY: [*laughing*] Evan. We used to see you all the time. Why did you ever leave?

EVAN: You know why I left. I was found wanting.

IVY: Perhaps we can change all that. I'll do some work on your behalf.

EVAN: I think you'll be wasting your time.

IVY: We'll see.

BEN: [*approaching* MONICA] How are you, Monica?

MONICA: Oh. Fine.

BEN: You're making a mistake.

[MONICA *turns to look at him.*]

Can you see Hugh in your father's place? Just think about it, Monica. You're very young. Hugh's very nice, but to survive around here you've got to have a bit more in the way of mettle.

MONICA: You're too late with your advice. And I don't thank you for it.

[*Pause.*]

Whatever Hugh lacks, I'm sure that I've got.

[LEO *comes to the front door.*]

IVY: Leo! Happy New Year.

LEO: Hello everyone. Happy everything. You look very nice, Mrs Hindmarsh. And I see you've got a nice touch of variety in your guest list.

IVY: Yes. How was the trip?

LEO: I don't know. I stayed home this afternoon, preening myself for the big event.

MONICA: Then who took the boat out?

LEO: Who do you think?

MONICA: No . . .

LEO: Hugh would be very disappointed to hear you say that, Monica. Nothing means more to a man than a bit of faith on the home front.

IVY: Hugh took the boat out without you?

LEO: I made him captain of the *Werriwa* and then went home and started a big search for my hair oil. Unsuccessfully, as it turned out. Rest easy. Hugh's got a good crew of river rats and he'll be fine.

[MONICA *heads for the door.*]

IVY: Monica, where are you going?

MONICA: Down to the boatshed.

LEO: Not in that dress. It'd be a tragedy. You sit down and have a drink and Hugh'll be here soon enough.

IVY: Yes, I think you should stay, Monica.

EVAN: I'll have a dance with you in the meantime, if you like.

MONICA: I thought you'd be there, Leo.

EVAN: The young lady's upset, Leo, and it's all your fault. Come and have a drink.

LEO: I've got some business to do with Mrs Hindmarsh.

EVAN: Who hasn't. This place will drive me mad.

LEO: This is for you.

[LEO *gives* IVY *a paper bag. She opens it and holds up four knives.*]

Some of your silver. It found its way down to my place under exceptional circumstances.

[IVY *stares at the silver.* MONICA *comes over and*

examines it.]

MONICA: We were missing four knives.

    [*She smiles at* LEO.]

  Thank you, Leo.

LEO: Am I forgiven for deserting Hugh?

MONICA: I'll think about it.

IVY: Thank you, Leo. Thank you very much.

LEO: It's my pleasure.

    [ADELA *appears at the top of the stairs.*]

ADELA: Have you started without me?

    [*They look up at her in silence.*]

LEO: Adela, that is a beautiful dress.

    [ADELA *comes down the stairs.*]

ADELA: Ooh, the compliments have started. I must get in on this. How nice not to have to scrounge! How very nice.

LEO: You don't have to scrounge.

ADELA: Happy New Year, Leo. And everyone. My God, look who's here. All sorts of people and Evan, too.

EVAN: I won't bite, Adela. You look too beautiful. I'm dazzled, I confess it.

ADELA: Now my head *is* turned.

    [*She takes out her cigarette holder and lights a cigarette.*]

BEN: Would you like a drink, Adela?

EVAN: He's woken up. Ben, I thought you were sulking.

ADELA: I'd *love* a drink. Thank you, Ben.

LEO: I must think seriously about asking you for a dance.

ADELA: Leo, I hate to see you begging. Thank you, Ben.

    [*She takes the drink from* BEN *and sips it.* IVY *has been watching this performance with a detached air.*]

IVY: Welcome to the party, Adela.

ADELA: Thank you, Mummy. Can I give you a hand with anything?

IVY: How nice of you to ask, but Monica and I have been in charge and it's all progressing beautifully.

ADELA: I should have come down earlier.

IVY: You did what you thought was right.

ADELA: Anyway, I'm sure you've all done a great job.

IVY: Thank you, Adela. You do have to smoke, don't you?

ADELA: Oh, of course. It's a gesture of . . . what? Defiance, I
    think.
MONICA: What are you defying?
    [*Fireworks send flashes of light from farther up the
    river.*]
ADELA: Oh, they've started the fireworks. How exciting.
    And what a pity we haven't got any.
LEO: I got some in for you, but I thought the rain would be
    a problem.
IVY: They're beautiful. Never mind the rain, Leo. We must
    put on our own show at midnight. After all, tonight
    is . . . what is it again?
BEN: Federation.
LEO: I'll bring them up from the boatshed later on.
IVY: Leo, I can't tell you how pleased I am to get that silver
    back.
LEO: You haven't been eating with your fingers, have you?
IVY: You know very well what I mean.
LEO: I can only guess.
    [EVAN *has joined* ADELA.]
EVAN: Who else is coming tonight?
ADELA: I thought you said I was dazzling.
EVAN: I've got to be practical.
ADELA: Why don't you just take things as they come?
EVAN: If there's one thing I don't need, one thing that would
    make me dangerously angry, it's a suggestion, no matter
    how slight, of any encouragement from you.
ADELA: It's the last thing I have in mind. But if I change, I'll
    let you know.
    [EVAN *glares at her.*]
    You *do* look dangerously angry. I must remember to be
    on my guard. Oh, what *beautiful* balloons! And the
    flowers! I can tell this is going to be a night of nights.
    Don't you agree?
    [BEN *joins them.*]
BEN: What's the matter, Evan? Still got no dancing partner?
    [HUGH *comes in the front door.*]
LEO: There he is. What'd I tell you?
    [MONICA *embraces* HUGH.]

MONICA: You didn't get hurt, did you?

HUGH: Of course not. Happy New Year, Mrs Hindmarsh, everyone.

ADELA: Hugh, where have you been?

HUGH: I took the *Werriwa* out on an excursion trip.

ADELA: Well done. What an adventure!

HUGH: It wasn't an adventure. It was hard work.

ADELA: Oh, of course.

HUGH: It's a sluggish old thing, the *Werriwa*, but when it gets a bit of gallop up it moves beautifully. You almost need a tug-boat to dock her, though. I thought we'd overshot the wharf, and then I thought we might take the wharf with us when the rope was popping the odd strand, but then it settled, like a dog when you give it its dinner. It was wonderful, though, out on the river. You know those willows, they're really beautiful. It's almost as if they've got caverns under them. They're like rooms in a house. A big house. A long house.

IVY: Yes, Hugh, that's very pleasing. Now, could I have everyone's attention, please. I have an announcement to make.

MONICA: Mummy, you're not going to —

IVY: Yes I am. I have great pleasure in announcing the engagement of my youngest daughter Monica to Mr Hugh Crane of...

HUGH: Goondiwindi.

IVY: Goondiwindi.

HUGH: I left when I was a baby.

IVY: Probably a wise move. Congratulations. And my blessing.

EVAN: [*shaking hands with* HUGH] Congratulations. And to you, Monica.

LEO: And from me, Hugh. This is a big day for you.

HUGH: Thanks. Thanks.

LEO: And to the youngest Hindmarsh.

IVY: To date.

LEO: Yes, of course.

[LEO *kisses* MONICA.]

MONICA: Thank you, Leo.

ADELA: [*to* IVY] This is all a bit sudden. Why wasn't I told?

IVY: Don't call it sudden, for God's sake. Now go and wish them well.

> [ADELA *goes over to* HUGH *and* MONICA.]

BEN: Are you planning that Hugh and Monica will run *Wombelano* with Leo as manager?

IVY: It's not up to me, Mr Bromley. If that's what Hugh and Monica and Leo want, then I'd be delighted.

BEN: They couldn't do it without Leo, could they?

IVY: I imagine they'd find his help invaluable.

ADELA: You two haven't wasted much time, have you? I knew something was on, but not this quickly.

HUGH: If people think it's happened quickly, then they probably won't say so at any great length.

ADELA: Oh, of course. Oh God, there I go, you're not . . . oh I won't ask. Look, let me just say how pleased I am and also express the hope that you won't take Monny away from us.

HUGH: I think we've decided to stay here, haven't we?

MONICA: For the first year, anyway. But Hugh, I don't really want to stay here for ever. Not in Sleepy Hollow. Are we agreed on that?

HUGH: Why don't we just see how we feel next year?

ADELA: Yes, Monny. I think we should all stay here, and you should start telling me now how *welcome* I'll be and how . . . *indispensable* I've become and that we'll all be happy here together and you, Hugh, should be devoting an hour each day to singing songs of praise for your sister-in-law-elect and stopping one in three people on the street and saying '*How* could we ever survive without Adela?' *And* reassuring Mummy and Livvie and Charles that they'll be almost as welcome as me.

MONICA: Della, of course you'll be welcome.

ADELA: Dear Monny, I know that.

MONICA: But we can't promise we'll stay longer than a year.

ADELA: Oh, but you must stay for ever. We should never entertain anything less.

HUGH: We can't promise that, Adela.

> [*Music can be heard from inside.* ADELA *looks at them*

searchingly.]

ADELA: I understand.

MONICA: Don't worry.

ADELA: I'm not worried. At worst it'll be a stay of execution.
At best, a paradise. I'll convert you. But in the meantime
you two must go in and dance. And we must all come and
watch you and say how awful it is to lose our precious
Monny, but how glad we are that it's Hugh she's chosen.

HUGH: We'll keep our side of that.

[HUGH *and* MONICA *go towards the drawing room.*
ADELA *watches them go.* HUGH *stops, turns, and looks
back at* ADELA.]

Of course you'll be welcome.

MONICA: Come on.

[MONICA *leads* HUGH *out.* ADELA *is lost in thought.*
LEO *puts his arm out and* IVY *takes it. He puts out his
other arm for* ADELA.]

IVY: Wake up, Adela.

ADELA: What? Oh.

[*She takes* LEO's *arm absently.*]

ADELA: You don't think I would ever become a useless old
retainer, do you?

IVY: You'd have company.

[*The three of them go inside, watched by* BEN *and*
EVAN.]

BEN: That Hindmarsh girl. Adela.

EVAN: Learmonth.

BEN: Adela Learmonth. You've got to say this: she looks
very pretty tonight.

[EVAN *picks up* ADELA's *cigarette case.*]

EVAN: Oh, she's always been pretty. Mind you, she works at
it. Those long hours at the mirror have paid off in later
life. But when you come down to it, pretty or not she's just
a pea-brained socialite.

BEN: You sound very bitter.

EVAN: Not at all.

[*He tosses the cigarette case back on to the table.*]

BEN: Didn't you get to her?

EVAN: I'm quite secure in my own mind about that subject.

BEN: Come on, tell me.

EVAN: No.

[BEN *paces over to the window.*]

BEN: You were scared of the old skipper, weren't you?

EVAN: He made life difficult when it came to a few minor details, such as my prospects. But you never showed your face here till he died, did you?

BEN: I wish I had. The old girl's driving me mad.

EVAN: She's restless. She's never liked it here.

BEN: What about if she leaves it to Hugh and Monica?

EVAN: Monica will then sell it herself.

BEN: Of course. Monica's never liked it here either. What am I worried about?

EVAN: You know that Leo will probably put in a bid.

BEN: Oh, I know that. *Wombelano.* I never would have got near it while the old Captain was still alive.

EVAN: It was all I could do to get near Adela.

BEN: How near?

EVAN: He never knew either.

[ADELA *comes in quietly to get her cigarette case. She picks it up, pauses, and listens, unseen.*]

BEN: He must have been a cunning old bloke, Captain Hindmarsh. He always ran a boat and made it pay. He got out of freight and into passengers at just the right time.

EVAN: Oh yes, he was cunning. And he never had two scruples to rub together. One time he took on this load of so-called 'free labourers' during the big shearers' strike. Then he put the word about and off he went. He tied up at Echuca for supplies, knowing full well he wouldn't get any farther, and he didn't even try to look surprised when the strikers dropped a couple of torches on his deck. Well of course the dockers cast him off because the wharf was in danger and all the 'free labourers' had to swim for it. One of them drowned, but the old boy got his insurance money, development capital from both colonial governments, and bought the *Werriwa*.

ADELA: Leo! Leo!

EVAN: Adela! Have you been here...?

ADELA: I'm having you thrown out, Evan. You're disgusting. Leo!

EVAN: I'm sorry you heard that, but you've got to realise this, Adela; your father was just a man. He did what was necessary for his survival. If you ever grow up you'll understand that.

ADELA: No! I won't hear any more!

EVAN: I'm not trying to blacken him. He wasn't any worse than most of the river rats.

ADELA: Oh, look at you, Evan! Look how you've turned out. You're seedy and corrupt and vulgar.

EVAN: I could cry. But I think I'll dance with your mother instead. Excuse me.

    [LEO *comes in.*]

ADELA: Leo! Thank God!

LEO: What's all the shouting about?

ADELA: I want you to throw Evan out. Immediately!

LEO: Now come on, Adela. I can't do that.

ADELA: Why not?

LEO: We're not schoolboys.

ADELA: He insulted my father! He's a horrible, horrible person!

BEN: [*laughing*] I could have told you that.

EVAN: What's it going to be, Leo? Swords or pistols?

LEO: Why don't you cool off on the verandah for a while?

EVAN: Eh?

LEO: Here. Give me your glass.

    [*He takes* EVAN's *glass and fills it.*]

    Now. You take this and go for a walk and we'll see you a bit later on.

EVAN: You're not serious.

LEO: I could well be.

    [EVAN *takes the glass.*]

BEN: Come on, Evan. You've upset the mistress of the house. We'll be back in a while.

EVAN: [*glaring at* LEO *and* ADELA] Seedy and corrupt and vulgar, eh?

BEN: Come on.

    [BEN *leads* EVAN *out on the verandah.* EVAN *sits on the*

swing seat and moodily sips his drink.]

ADELA: Thank you, Leo. He said such awful things about
    my father. Awful.

LEO: Why did you call me?

ADELA: I was upset. I wanted you here.

LEO: Why me?

    [*She looks at him.*]

ADELA: I don't know.

    [*Pause.*]

  Yes, I do. Good God.

    [ADELA's *jaw drops. She stares at* LEO *in wonder and he
    looks steadily at her.*]

BEN: You know what? I think she's keen on Mulcahy.

EVAN: Yes.

BEN: You're his business partner . . .

EVAN: Some of the time.

BEN: Sure, sure. But you must know what he gets up to.

EVAN: Yes.

BEN: And you must know where the evidence is kept.

EVAN: Yes.

BEN: Where?

EVAN: The branding irons are in his boatshed. He's going to
    take his last load across tomorrow.

BEN: But the border tax ends at midnight.

EVAN: This is nothing to do with the border tax.

BEN: So it's straight-out cattle-stealing?

EVAN: Yes.

BEN: And Mulcahy knows it is.

EVAN: He turns a blind eye. I believe he thinks it's just
    smuggling.

BEN: That's as good as being guilty.

EVAN: There's no mud on me.

BEN: Of course not. Let's go.

    [EVAN *hesitates, then drains his glass. He and* BEN
    leave.

      HUGH *and* MONICA *dance in through the doorway.
    They whirl around the room and then out the front
    door. They dance across the verandah and collapse
    laughing into the swing seat.* LEO *does a few dance*

steps and then stops and smiles at ADELA. *She smiles at him.* HUGH *finds he has been sitting on* ADELA's *hoop. He stands up and puts the hoop behind the seat and then sits down again.* LEO *puts his arms out, indicating that they should dance.* ADELA *throws her cigarette case on the table. She comes across, holding out her arms, and they start to dance. The fireworks resume.*]

HUGH: Look at that. The river could almost be on fire.

MONICA: It's beautiful. We must buy some fireworks and celebrate the first of each month.

HUGH: How about the first of each week?

MONICA: I think we'd get sick of that.

HUGH: I don't think we'll ever get sick of anything.

[*They kiss.* LEO *and* ADELA *slow down and stop. They kiss and then look closely at each other.* HUGH *and* MONICA *watch the fireworks.*]

LEO: I want you to tell me something.

ADELA: Anything I can.

LEO: Why now?

ADELA: You had to wait for me to grow up. I must say you were very patient. You see, it's not that I disapprove of adult life. It's just that it's never looked like much fun.

LEO: It isn't.

ADELA: Perhaps the time has come to stop having fun.

LEO: We may be able to dredge up a few light moments here and there.

ADELA: I think there's every chance.

LEO: I still don't believe it.

ADELA: Don't worry. It's not a dream. The past was a dream.

LEO: This is not even dream-like?

ADELA: Not even that.

LEO: You're very sure.

ADELA: Oh, yes.

LEO: Then I believe you.

ADELA: Now it's my turn. I want to ask you something.

LEO: Anything.

ADELA: Will you do what is necessary for my survival?

LEO: Do I have to?

ADELA: Yes, and with good grace, too.

LEO: I'll give you all the grace I've got.
  [*They kiss.*]

HUGH: It's beautiful here. I really love it now. *Wombelano.*
  What does that mean?

MONICA: Beach.

HUGH: Beach? But we're two hundred miles and more from
  the sea.

MONICA: We'll still get a good price for it.

HUGH: Monica! We agreed not to talk about that for now.

MONICA: Yes. I'm sorry.

HUGH: We're going to give this place every chance. Do you
  understand?

MONICA: Yes.

ADELA: [*running her hand down* LEO's *face*] I don't believe
  in dreams because my own are so predictable. I am
  always, and I do really mean *always*, running through a
  forest. What my objective is, whether it's getting away
  from a bear or catching the train to Albury, I have never
  known.

LEO: Let's see if we can make that running through a
  vineyard.

ADELA: Yes, but towards what?

LEO: Modesty prevents . . .
  [*They embrace.* HUGH *looks at* MONICA. *The fireworks
  stop and it starts to rain again.*]

HUGH: I've got a feeling that in your single-minded way you
  really do love me.

MONICA: Could be.
  [*She kisses him.* CHARLES *wheels himself into the room,
  stopping when he sees* LEO *and* ADELA. *They break
  apart and stare at him.* CHARLES *smiles.*]

CHARLES: At last.

ADELA: Yes.
  [OLIVIA *bustles in.*]

OLIVIA: Charles, what are you doing?

CHARLES: Giving my best wishes to the engaged couple.

OLIVIA: They're outside, looking at the fireworks, which is
  where we should be.

CHARLES: Are they engaged?

OLIVIA: Of course they are.

LEO: I'd say so.

ADELA: Oh. Definitely.

OLIVIA: Come on, you wanted to see the fireworks.

CHARLES: Just a minute, Livvie. I want to tell Adela that I love her very much and that I wish her all the best for her future happiness.

OLIVIA: What an extraordinary thing to say.

ADELA: Thank you, Charles. I love you very much, too.
   [*She kisses him.*]

OLIVIA: Well, I'm going out to watch the fireworks.
   [CHARLES *grabs* OLIVIA's *arm.*]

CHARLES: Livvie. I didn't mean to hurt you.

OLIVIA: How was I hurt? You've all gone mad. But that doesn't hurt me at all.

CHARLES: Will you come out to the verandah with me?

OLIVIA: All right.
   [OLIVIA *takes up her position behind the wheelchair and looks around at the other three.*]

ADELA: We're not mad, Livvie. And we're not drunk. And we all love you.
   [OLIVIA *shakes her head. She wheels* CHARLES *towards the door.* IVY *comes in.*]

IVY: That blasted rain. I'm sick of it. Now it's pouring down and I'm sure we're in for a flood. Have you seen the river? It's about to burst. What a thing to happen on New Year's Eve.

ADELA: Calm down, Mummy. There's nothing we can do about it.

IVY: Why don't they build a dam? Why must we suffer every time there's a flood? It really is too much to bear.

LEO: No use getting upset. I've got something more important to announce.

ADELA: Oh not yet, Leo. Please.

LEO: Why not?

ADELA: I'd be too embarrassed.

LEO: I'll leave it to you, then.

ADELA: That's what I'd like.

IVY: [*turning to* OLIVIA] What's all this? What's she embarrassed about now?

OLIVIA: I don't know. Ask Charles.

CHARLES: I'd be too embarrassed.

[IVY *stares at* LEO *and* ADELA. *She then turns to* OLIVIA.]

IVY: Would you get me a drink, please Livvie.

[OLIVIA *goes over to the punch.* HUGH *and* MONICA *run in from the verandah.*]

HUGH: It's pouring! It's like a waterfall.

MONICA: I just hope we haven't got anything in the boatshed.

HUGH: Should I go down and look?

MONICA: No! Don't you dare go out again. Let's forget it. This is a party and we should all be dancing. Shall we? [*She turns to* HUGH *who hesitates.*]

IVY: Go ahead and dance. What else can we do? [*They start to dance.* ADELA *turns to* LEO, *then they too dance.*]

CHARLES: Two elegant couples. And they look so happy. [IVY *stares hard at* ADELA *and* LEO. *She gulps down some more punch.*]

  Don't you think it's a pleasing sight?

IVY: Adela and Leo seem very friendly.

CHARLES: They're old friends.

IVY: They seem more than friends tonight.

CHARLES: They probably are.

[IVY *stares at* CHARLES *and then at* ADELA.]

IVY: Couldn't be. Couldn't be.

OLIVIA: Mummy, what on earth are you babbling about?

IVY: I was talking to myself.

[BEN *and* EVAN *burst in the front door.*]

BEN: The boatshed's in trouble.

EVAN: You should see the river. Have you got anything down there? We'd better bring it up now.

MONICA: The fireworks! Are they down there?

LEO: Yes.

MONICA: Oh, Leo, please bring them up. It'd be such a pity to lose them. Please, Leo. Ple-eease.

LEO: You've been saying that for twenty years.

MONICA: Oh come on, surely my voice is different. Now will you get them?

LEO: All right. I've got a few barrels of stuff down there. I'll bring them up.

MONICA: Thank you, Leo.

BEN: We'll give you a hand.

LEO: Will you?

EVAN: Of course.

[LEO *watches them warily.*]

OLIVIA: I'll get the oilskins for you.

[*She rushes out.*]

HUGH: One for me, too, Livvie.

OLIVIA: [*off*] Right.

ADELA: [*to* LEO] Won't it be dangerous? If the boatshed is in danger, then so will you be.

LEO: I don't think there'll be a flood tonight. [*Indicating* BEN *and* EVAN] This pair have had too much excitement.

ADELA: Don't you risk anything, will you?

IVY: Leo will be back soon, Adela.

ADELA: Why tell me, Mummy?

IVY: You seem the most concerned.

ADELA: I am concerned. For humanity.

LEO: Thank you very much.

[OLIVIA *comes back with the oilskins which* LEO, HUGH, BEN *and* EVAN *put on.*]

ADELA: You do have to go down, do you?

LEO: I think so.

BEN: Come on, we'd better hurry.

IVY: Monica, go and tell them to stop playing that music.

[MONICA *goes out.*]

Why we have to live beside a river I don't know.

BEN: It must be by choice.

EVAN: Let's go.

[EVAN, BEN, LEO *and* HUGH *go out the front door. The music stops.* MONICA *comes back in.* ADELA *looks around at the others. There is silence.* ADELA *goes out the front door. She stands on the verandah and looks down at the river.*]

CHARLES: Mother. I think you're ready to go.

IVY: Do you think so?

CHARLES: That's what you said you wanted.

IVY: Yes, but a few things have happened since.

CHARLES: Such as?

IVY: You.

CHARLES: Don't worry about me. I'll stay on here and I think I'll be made to feel welcome.

MONICA: Of course you will, Charles.

IVY: Where do you think I should be off-loaded?

MONICA: Mummy, don't talk like that, please.

CHARLES: You and Olivia should go on a trip around the world and then live in Melbourne.

IVY: How can I be sure *Wombelano* will be in good hands? How can I be sure you'll be looked after?

CHARLES: I'll guarantee both jobs. The simple fact is that it's time for you to retire in favour of your children. It's nothing to do with off-loading or even competence. It's just an acknowledgement of the passing of time. Above all, it's to do with you. You should be happy in what you do.

IVY: So that's come back to haunt me.

OLIVIA: It is true, though, Mummy.

IVY: Oh, I don't know. I don't think I'll ever decide. Is there any need to, when all is said and done?

CHARLES: I believe so, yes.

[IVY *wanders over and studies the indoor garden.* LEO *rolls a barrel up on to the verandah.* ADELA *has been waiting for him.* LEO *leans over and kisses her quickly, then leaves.* ADELA *paces up and down with suppressed excitement.* LEO *hurries back in, kisses her again, and hurries off.* EVAN *comes up next with his barrel.* ADELA *walks over to sit on the swing seat as* EVAN *rolls his barrel onto the verandah, his oilskins wet and glistening. He looks at* ADELA, *who appears not to notice him. He goes.* HUGH *rolls up his barrel.*]

HUGH: I've been meaning to get you alone.

ADELA: Aren't you busy at present?

HUGH: Yes, but I want to tell you something.

ADELA: I'm not in a listening mood. Please don't think me
    abrupt. I'm all full up, and that is the truth.
HUGH: I just want to say I'm in some sense beholden to you.
    And a little bit overcome with admiration for you. I'll
    always do whatever you want. Keep that in mind, will
    you?
ADELA: Oh, what dangerous and *thrilling* power you've
    given me. It could go to my head and then we could blow
    up the world together. But I am only able to give it half a
    mind, if that, because I'm in love, do you hear, I'm in
    love. I, Adela Learmonth, considered silly and immature
    by countless impartial observers, am in love. I can't ever
    use my power over you because I am in love. Thank you
    for your offer. Thank you for your time.
        [HUGH *stares at her.* MONICA *comes out on to the
        verandah.*]
MONICA: Shouldn't we give them a hand somehow?
        [ADELA *turns and looks at her.*]
ADELA: I don't want to get wet. [*Going over to the swing
    seat*] I want to sit here and dream, and my dream will be
    about a girl — no, a woman — running through a
    vineyard above a smooth-flowing river.
MONICA: What's this?
HUGH: I think she's in love.
        [HUGH *goes.* MONICA *looks across at* ADELA, *who rocks
        contentedly.* IVY *turns from the garden under the stairs
        and looks at* CHARLES *and* OLIVIA.]
IVY: I'll never make a decision, now that you've confused
    me. You think I should leave *Wombelano* to all of you?
CHARLES: No. Just one.
IVY: Monica?
CHARLES: Adela.
IVY: Oh, Charles! And I thought you were making sense at
    last.
OLIVIA: I don't think you're joking, are you Charles?
CHARLES: No, I'm not.
IVY: It's a ridiculous suggestion.
OLIVIA: Tell me, Charles: what has Adela done for you?
CHARLES: Not nearly as much as you, Livvie, and I'm sad to

hear you ask that.

OLIVIA: I'm sad, too.

CHARLES: Remember this, Mother. Monica only wants the place so she can sell it.

[*He wheels himself over to the front door.*]

It's stopped raining. I think I'll go out and see how they're going.

[OLIVIA *comes over and wheels him out.* IVY *lingers, contemplating the garden, deep in thought. Then she follows them out on to the verandah.* BEN *rolls up his barrel. It rattles noisily.*]

IVY: It's stopped raining, Mr Bromley. I think we're out of danger, thank you.

BEN: That's interesting. Doesn't sound like fireworks.

[LEO *rolls up a barrel.*]

LEO: This is the last lot now.

IVY: Thank you, Leo. You've saved us yet again.

BEN: Has he now? That's commendable.

IVY: Thank you, too, Mr Bromley.

BEN: I think Leo's saved himself as well.

[HUGH *and* EVAN *roll their barrels up.*]

HUGH: That's it.

IVY: What do you mean, Leo's saved himself?

BEN: I mean he hasn't neglected his own welfare.

LEO: What is it now, Bromley?

BEN: I'll show you.

[*He empties the barrel on to the verandah. It is full of branding irons.* LEO *picks one up and examines it.*]

MONICA: What are they?

BEN: Branding irons. Or, rather, re-branding irons. For changing the brand on cattle. Ever been down to the river at night? If you're lucky you'll catch your neighbour here on his punt.

LEO: I do believe you're trying to provoke something.

IVY: What do you mean, Mr Bromley?

LEO: Everyone takes cattle across the river.

BEN: Don't be too quick. That's not the point. You don't just take cattle across. You take stolen cattle, which are re-branded on the other side.

LEO: I don't ask to see a bloodline.

BEN: How did these irons come to be in your boatshed?

LEO: It's not my boatshed. I share it with the Hindmarshes.

BEN: You're not suggesting Mrs Hindmarsh is a cattle thief?

LEO: No.

BEN: How did they get there?

LEO: I don't know.

BEN: Who's going to believe that?

LEO: People who believe in me, I expect.

BEN: And who comprises this brave little band?

ADELA: [*raising her hand*] I'll put my name down.

BEN: That's quite a coup. But I notice Mrs Hindmarsh is silent. Perhaps she's disillusioned with this man of the world, this adventurer who's trying to present himself as the manager of *Wombelano*.

IVY: Oh no, Leo's not going to be the manager. I didn't want him to...it's been kept in the...I'm sorry, Leo, to bring this up.

BEN: *Wombelano*'s been kept in the family, has it? For Hugh and Monica?

HUGH: Now look, Bromley, Mrs Hindmarsh doesn't have to undergo this interrogation. What right have you got to pose as some kind of all-seeing magistrate?

BEN: Just the normal creditor's rights.

MONICA: We won't be in debt any more if we sell the *Werriwa*.

HUGH: Monica!

MONICA: Well, what use is it? It's a floating tombstone.

CHARLES: Are you thinking hard, mother?

IVY: Yes, Charles. Yes. Yes.

EVAN: I don't think you're getting anywhere, Ben. Leo seems to have found some kind of niche here, some station in life between dogsbody and high priest.

BEN: He's a thief.

EVAN: Now, now.

BEN: Men work hard to build up their herds and along comess Mulcahy.

LEO: Careful now.

BEN: Perhaps having a father who was a gaolbird had something to do with it. Perhaps there's something in this theory about the bad seed.

[LEO *raises his branding iron.*]

LEO: Perhaps you'd like to defend yourself.

[LEO *tosses a branding iron to* BEN.]

BEN: I think we're getting to this river rat. He seems upset.

IVY: Leo, you're not proposing to fight Mr Bromley, are you?

LEO: Not at all. But I think he deserves some form of punishment.

BEN: Why's that?

LEO: Who picked up the excursion people the day Charles was hurt? I heard it was a boat recently acquired by a friend of yours. And I heard he was grateful to you for putting a bit of business his way.

[BEN *swings his iron at* LEO, *who ducks.* BEN *swings again.* HUGH *blocks the blow with an iron.* BEN *stares at him, amazed.*]

HUGH: Come on now. You're not getting anywhere.

EVAN: Let them have a go, Hugh.

IVY: Evan, how can you encourage this behaviour? I thought you were better than that.

EVAN: Not me.

IVY: Hugh! Stop them!

LEO: Stand back, Hugh. Let Bromley work it out of himself.

[MONICA *pulls* HUGH *back.* BEN *hesitates.*]

LEO: I think it's all over for you, Ben. This place has secrets you'll never get near. If it goes down, it'll do so in its own wilful way. And it'll all happen behind doors that are closed to you.

EVAN: I can vouch for that, Ben.

LEO: Give up, old son. It just hasn't panned out the right way. You're not equal to it, you haven't got the temperament. Not to mention the ability. Perhaps your own parents went wrong in some strange way.

[BEN *hurls himself at* LEO, *swinging his iron.* LEO *blocks the blows, one after the other.* ADELA *rushes forward.*]

ADELA: Stop it! Stop it! You stay back! And put that iron

down.

BEN: You've got yourself a second, Mulcahy. Tell her it's seconds out now.

ADELA: Will you please leave this property.

BEN: This is nothing to do with you, Adela.

ADELA: Yes it is! I love him! I love him!

[*There is silence.*]

EVAN: Hull-o...

IVY: Adela...

EVAN: You can't keep a good woman down.

[LEO *lowers his iron.* BEN *swings at him, but* HUGH *blocks the blow.*]

HUGH: That's all for now.

[BEN *throws* HUGH *off and advances on* LEO.]

OLIVIA: Oh, somebody stop them!

[CHARLES *picks up the hoop.*]

CHARLES: Hugh.

[CHARLES *tosses the hoop to* HUGH, *who catches it.* BEN *swings at* LEO, *who blocks the blows.* BEN *squares off for another go, but* HUGH *drops the hoop over him and jerks him back.* BEN *falls over with a crash.*]

MONICA: Well done, Hugh.

[LEO *comes over and picks up* BEN's *iron.* ADELA *snatches up her hoop.*]

ADELA: Thank you, Hugh, even though you broke my hoop.

HUGH: It's only a small fracture.

ADELA: Yes, I suppose so. And Leo's all right.

LEO: Which is the main thing, I hope.

ADELA: By a whisker.

[*She kisses him.*]

MONICA: You'd better get Ben home, Evan.

EVAN: *I'd* better get him home? I came here for a party.

ADELA: There's no party here. Especially not for you.

EVAN: Listen to that. I've been cut down in my prime. Well, come on, Ben. We might do better on the bridge. Can I keep the oilskins for now?

MONICA: Oh, of course you can, Evan.

ADELA: They suit you.

EVAN: Goodnight, Mrs Hindmarsh. And please accept my

condolences.

IVY: For what?

EVAN: You can't be overjoyed with Adela's apparent choice.
[IVY *hesitates.*]

BEN: [*getting to his feet*] She doesn't look overjoyed.

OLIVIA: Come inside and lie down, Mummy. The party
mood seems to have gone — not that I held out much
hope in the first place.

BEN: That allegation Leo made. There's no proof, Mrs
Hindmarsh. You have my word on that.
[*Pause.*]
Is that what you're thinking about?

IVY: No.

MONICA: Mummy, what is it?

IVY: Mr Bromley's right. I'm not overjoyed. But I have come
to my senses. After thirty-six years of justifiable reluctance
I have to admit something. And I don't do it in any spirit
of ecstasy. Adela is the heart of *Wombelano* and I am
patently not. For better or worse, the place is hers.

MONICA: Oh Mummy, stop and think!
[*They look at* ADELA. *She is stunned. She clutches her
hoop tightly. Fade out.*]

END OF ACT THREE

ACT FOUR

A View of the River

May 1901. Afternoon.

The gingham cloth is on the table. ADELA, *who is pregnant, sits on the swing seat mending her hoop with twine.*

LEO *comes in from the vineyard holding a bunch of grapes.*

LEO: Don't tell me that's gone again.

ADELA: [*putting the hoop down*] I don't mind. I enjoy fixing it. [*As* LEO *hands her the grapes*] Not more grapes. When are people going to start drinking wine?

LEO: That's the last of the Hermitage.

ADELA: I bet they're full of sugar.

LEO: You could use them in tea. Might be a way of selling them.

[*He feels her stomach.*]

No kicks?

ADELA: No.

LEO: No bruises?

ADELA: Not this century.

LEO: Now *that's* the right attitude. Any news of the day?

ADELA: I got a letter from Mummy and Olivia. They're marauding around Venice at present.

LEO: I bet they're loving it.

ADELA: Yes, the letter was very much along the lines of 'Why didn't we do this years ago?'

LEO: Good for them.

ADELA: I heard some other news. Ben Bromley's running for Parliament.

LEO: I'm not surprised. Those people think they're born to rule.

ADELA: But Bromley's no one much.

LEO: Exactly.

ADELA: What did you do today?

LEO: I sold the *Werriwa*.

79

ADELA: Finally.

LEO: Yes.

ADELA: What a relief.

LEO: I think I'll go in and wash up.

> [*He kisses her.*]

Tell me if you get any kicks.

ADELA: I'll scream. Come back soon, won't you?

LEO: Are you feeling frightened?

ADELA: No, just in need of a little comforting.

LEO: Give me ten minutes. And then we'll have a glass of wine out here.

ADELA: Yes, we must set an example.

LEO: It's our duty. Back straight.

> [ADELA *sits up straight. They smile at each other and* LEO *goes upstairs.* ADELA *goes to pick up the hoop and then stops.* BEN *comes up.*]

BEN: Hello, Adela.

ADELA: I think it's time for you to go.

BEN: You can forget all that. I've left my firm. They ask too much of their employees. And as far as I'm personally concerned you can keep *Wombelano*.

ADELA: I never let go.

BEN: So. It's Mrs Adela Mulcahy, mistress of all you survey. You certainly fought for what you wanted.

ADELA: I don't own the river. What do you want?

BEN: As you know, I'm canvassing votes and aligning my philosophy with the electorate's. Of course, it'll depend on your ability to put politics above personalities.

ADELA: I see a major struggle ahead.

BEN: Ah, come on, Adela, I'm just trying to make a bloody living. I'll leave you my pamphlet anyway.

ADELA: Does it contain your biography? Perhaps an account of what really happened the day of Charles's accident.

BEN: You're suggesting I was involved?

ADELA: Yes.

BEN: Say it in public. I've got a lawyer who'll sue you for libel and take this place off you.

ADELA: I'm saying it to you.

BEN: You'll keep those thoughts to yourself.

ADELA: You be careful, too.

BEN: What can you do? You people never do anything.

ADELA: Yes, but we're still here. We're still alive. I'd still be careful, if I were you.

[BEN *goes.* ADELA *crumples up his pamphlet as she watches him go.* FRANCES *wheels* CHARLES *out.*]

CHARLES: So this is where you hide.

ADELA: I like the view of the river. How are you?

CHARLES: Bursting with good deeds yet unborn. I'm going to Sydney tomorrow, to stay with Hugh and Monica for a while.

ADELA: But I can't take you.

CHARLES: Frances and I will manage, won't we Frances?

FRANCES: I'm confident.

CHARLES: Then I am, too.

FRANCES: I'll be back in ten minutes. Then it's time for a long walk. Understand?

CHARLES: [*as* FRANCES *leaves*] My teeth are already gritted. You could say you'll miss me.

ADELA: You'll be well cared for by Hugh and Monica.

CHARLES: Not Hugh. He's writing a novel.

ADELA: Really. What's it called?

CHARLES: 'Walk Across the River'.

ADELA: He was forever quoting the Bible.

CHARLES: He hasn't got much imagination. Apparently the heroine is called Ada.

ADELA: She sounds ghastly.

CHARLES: You look a bit broody.

ADELA: I think it's understandable. Actually, I was feeling a little sad. The *Werriwa*'s been sold.

CHARLES: It had to happen.

ADELA: Yes, but I can't help feeling sad.

CHARLES: You shouldn't. The *Werriwa*'s not worth it, compared to your achievements.

ADELA: That's it. I don't feel sad about the *Werriwa*. I feel sad about my achievements.

CHARLES: I don't see how you could possibly be disappointed.

ADELA: I can.

CHARLES: You're wrong. Do you understand? Wrong.

ADELA: I'm not wrong.

CHARLES: Why are you sad? What conceivable reason could you have?

ADELA: I've failed.

CHARLES: That's nonsense.

ADELA: It's not. I've failed.

CHARLES: Failed at what?

ADELA: I've failed in my life. I've failed! I don't know what I was supposed to do, the example I was set was too vague, there were too many dreams without any point, but *this* I do know, about *this* I am not vague, I have failed. But one thing I want you to tell me, one thing alone. What was I supposed to do? *What was I supposed to do? What was wanted of me?*

CHARLES: Adela, you're the one who's succeeded.

ADELA: What? Succeeded?

CHARLES: I mean it. You fought for your life and won.

ADELA: Won what?

CHARLES: For one thing, you succeeded in finding your level. You're happy in what you do.

ADELA: But isn't that an easy way out? God, there's such a chill in my head.

CHARLES: No, Adela. It's better than spending your life charging up and down the river to no good purpose. Don't raise people's expectations, our father always said. It's a very dangerous thing to do. If you do and then it doesn't work out, they'll turn on you with hatred. Do you agree?

ADELA: I suppose it makes sense.

CHARLES: Do you hate our father?

ADELA: Never. I couldn't.

CHARLES: Then he didn't raise your expectations too high, did he?

ADELA: Perhaps not in any specific way. Perhaps not at all. I don't know. Yes, he did. I know he did. He inspired such love and yes, such expectations, just by example.

CHARLES: He couldn't help that.

ADELA: If I knew what was wanted, wanted of me, then I'd

be quiet inside for the first time in my life.

CHARLES: Look at the way we've all turned out. And then look at yourself. You must see it, Adela. You must see that you're a success.

ADELA: The way I've turned out.

CHARLES: Yes. And the rest of us. The way we've turned out. You're the one with the land and the child.

ADELA: Yes.

CHARLES: You see?

ADELA: Perhaps you're right. It's gone now. My body feels warm.

[ADELA *clutches her back.*]

CHARLES: Did you get a little kick?

ADELA: No, it's just my back. The doctor said while thirty-six is not too old, it's not too young, either. I didn't have the heart to tell him I just turned thirty-seven.

CHARLES: [*grasping her hand.*] My darling Adela.

[*She smiles at him.*]

ADELA: If you go now you'll leave me in peace.

[*He smiles at her and then wheels himself off.* ADELA *grimaces, looks up deep in thought and then smiles wanly, gazing down at the river. A feeling of peace settles on her. She picks up her hoop. Fade out.*]

THE END

*Suzette Williams and Diane Craig as Ellen and Toby in
the Melbourne Theatre Company production. Photo by
David Parker*

THE MARGINAL FARM

*Terence Donovan as Marshal in the Melbourne Theatre
Company production. Photo by David Parker*

The Marginal Farm was first performed by the Melbourne Theatre Company at the Russell Street Theatre, Melbourne, on 2 November 1983 with the following cast:

TOBY	Diane Craig
JAMES	Robert van Mackelenberg
ELLEN	Suzette Williams
TAKA	Justine Saunders
PHILIP	Chris Connelly
MARSHAL	Terence Donovan
ILLY	Monroe Reimers

Designed by Richard Roberts
Directed by Aarne Neeme

CHARACTERS

TOBY, real name Elspeth Parks, a pale, attractive Australian governess in her late thirties

JAMES, a handsome, erratic English pilot in his early thirties.

ELLEN, a seventeen year-old Australian girl living in Fiji

PHILIP, a seventeen year-old Australian boy living in Fiji

TAKA, a Fijian girl in her mid-twenties, housekeeper

MARSHAL, a vigorous Australian in his late fifties, Field Officer with the Colonial Sugar Refining Company (CSR)

ILLY, a strongly built Fijian Indian farm worker and sometime tourist guide in his mid-thirties

SETTING

Fiji in the 1950s and 1960s.

The verandah and yard of Marshal's house outside Lautoka. The verandah is on the left, with steps leading down to the yard. At the back is a shed.

Along the right is a wooden doorway with a sign above it advertising Lukbo soft drinks. This area is intended for use in the scenes set in Lautoka. Otherwise, it is just part of the yard. There is a small bench near the doorway.

The exit right leads out to the road. Near this exit is a faded 1930s pump-style petrol bowser coloured yellow and red.

The house is on a hill overlooking a valley in sugar cane country.

NOTE

Fiji became independent in 1970.

Nadi is pronounced *Nandy*; Sigatoka is pronounced *Singatoeka*. In the period of the play the population of Fiji was about 500,000. The Fijians made up about forty-five per cent of the population; the Indians forty-five per cent; the whites ten per cent.

ACT ONE

TOBY *sits on her suitcase on the wharf at Lautoka. She is playing patience on the top of a larger suitcase. It is a hot morning. She wears a white dress and a sun hat.*
JAMES *appears, holding two ice creams.*

JAMES: Oh, hello. You must be Elspeth . . . or is it Toby?
TOBY: Both.
JAMES: [*handing her an ice cream*] This is for you. It's a fairly minor form of atonement for being late. Have you been waiting long?
    [TOBY *glances at the cards.*]
It's Fiji time, you know. The driver didn't have the car ready. Now he's off to do the shopping. My name's James, by the way. Or Jim. Jimmy Witts.
TOBY: How do you do. I expected an older man. With a different name.
JAMES: Marshal's busy, sends his apologies, will crack a bottle at six to welcome you, etcetera. Toby's a nickname, is it?
TOBY: Originally, yes. Now it's acquired semi-legal status.
JAMES: How did you get it?
    [TOBY *gives him a battered smile.*]
You've been called on to explain that before?
    [*She nods.*]
Just once more. I'm a pilot. I'll promise to memorise your explanation and then write it in the sky in English, Fijian and Hindi. You'll never be bothered again.
TOBY: All right. My father thought I looked like a Toby jug when he first saw me. He was soon to be proved wrong by the march of time, but the name stuck. I suppose if I hang around long enough I'll deserve it again.
JAMES: Two weeks in Fiji ought to do it. Must be awkward sometimes, having a boy's name. People might make mistakes.
TOBY: Oh, they soon get the idea that I'm a girl.
JAMES: Yeah, I'd — yeah. But in the meantime, between

jugs, you're a governess.

TOBY: A governess. Oh, yes. Gosh. It sounds better than teacher. But perhaps it's a little inappropriately grand. I only got the job through corruption and nepotism. My Uncle Billy is an old friend of Marshal's and, dot dot dot, I was sent for. But that doesn't explain who you are and why you're here.

JAMES: Oh ... I'm a house-guest of Marshal's; I joined the R.A.F. in 1946, which was a bit anti-climactic, and, then, dot dot dot, here I am. I'm English — but then you probably guessed that.

TOBY: Oh, gosh yes.

JAMES: Would you like to go for a walk, see a bit of Lautoka?

TOBY: I've ... had a bit of a peek here and there, from the deck of the boat and so on, and ... well, I'm not in a Lautoka-viewing frame of mind. It's probably very nice. And I'm sure I'll get to see it before too long. But I just haven't got the urge, you know?

JAMES: Of course. You must be awfully hot. Why don't we seek out a cool hotel and have a beer or two? Unless of course you're a Muslim.

TOBY: On the contrary, I'm a member of the Labor Party.

JAMES: And they ...

TOBY: They drink.

JAMES: Then shall we go?

TOBY: No thank you.

JAMES: No?

TOBY: No. I mean, let me make this quite clear. I've arrived in Fiji determined to live life to the full. But I feel it behoves me to arrive sober and governess-like. Do you have any barley sugar?

JAMES: I'm afraid not. Cigarette?

TOBY: Not before lunch, thank you.

[JAMES *studies her.*]

JAMES: You give the impression of being someone who knows her own mind.

TOBY: Do I? Oh ...

[TOBY *ponders this.*]

JAMES: I wouldn't worry too much about being governess-like. I think you'll find Fiji pretty casual. It's the sort of place where you can have a good time. You are interested in having a good time, are you?

TOBY: Oh, absolutely. I'm almost obsessed about having a good time. And I won't be bought off, either.

JAMES: Then why don't you reconsider and we'll go and have a drink?

TOBY: No thank you.

JAMES: Here's the car now. Let me take your bags.

TOBY: We're going to Marshal's place, the Field Office, is that right?

JAMES: Of course. Now look. Don't worry about anything. I was once classified S.I.T. by protective mothers.

[TOBY *inclines her head.*]

Safe In Taxis.

[*He has picked up the suitcases and motions her ahead of him.*]

TOBY: That doesn't sound like a compliment.

JAMES: No. But then this isn't a taxi.

TOBY: Oh gosh.

JAMES: Yes.

[*They have gone.* ELLEN *wanders out on to the verandah. She is blowing a dandelion.*]

ELLEN: That's *not* what I want. And I *don't* like that. That's *not* what I'll do. And I *don't* care for you. And . . . you're *useless*.

[*She throws the stem away.*]

But then. What *do* you want? Oh. Well. Not sure. Not sure.

[TAKA *comes out on to the verandah.*]

TAKA: That was a long conversation.

ELLEN: What?

TAKA: You were talking to yourself again.

ELLEN: Oh yes. Yes.

TAKA: Do you find yourself a good conversationalist?

ELLEN: Yes, Taka. I suppose so.

TAKA: I wish you would find in others what you find in yourself.

[TAKA *starts mopping the verandah floor and* ELLEN

moves down the steps.]

ELLEN: You're being a bit severe on that poor old verandah.

TAKA: We're having drinks later this afternoon for the new arrival.

ELLEN: Who?

TAKA: Your governess. Remember? The lady who's coming here to teach you and Philip.

ELLEN: Oh, *her*. God, can you imagine it? A governess! They'll try anything. Won't do any good. Only trouble is, it'll ruin the summer. There'll be talk of hard work, yes, but *good* work and and ... *improvement* ... your *attitude* is all-important. *My* attitude? Yes, for the *growth* of your mind, for it is indeed a wonderful thing to behold the *progress* ... the progress ...

TAKA: Ellen, I wish you would talk to me instead of to yourself.

ELLEN: Oh yes. I'm sorry, Taka. It's hot, isn't it? It's hot. Yes, it is that. She won't last a week, this governess. She'll pack up her Shakespeare and her fan, she'll have a fan, I'm sure, and a scrofulous copy of *Richard the Second*, I'm sure ... where's Philip?

TAKA: He's coming.

ELLEN: It's hot, isn't it hot? There's going to be a storm, I can feel a storm. Oh, I know she's going to be ghastly. And what a winning way to spend the summer. They're going to have to call off the whole thing. It'll be too hot to hold a pen, I just know.

TAKA: You should have passed your exams.

ELLEN: Oh yes. Oh yes. The fault is here. The fault is in me. But there will be improvement, and a better person will emerge. A well rounded personality. There will be no, no 'lack of serious application' or indeed any 'serious lack of application'. Oh no. Oh no. She will 'work to full capacity', wasn't that it? Or something about 'potential'. Was the 'potential' being, was it 'exploited'. 'Exploited'? Can that be right? Do you 'exploit' potential?

TAKA: I don't know, Ellen.

ELLEN: Don't you read my report cards? I thought everyone did. They're very well written, you know. Lots of good punchy stuff.

TAKA: Here they come now. You be good.

ELLEN: Oh, I'll be good.

TAKA: Ellen . . .

ELLEN: You go and fix yourself up. I'll run the shop here. Go on, Taka.

TAKA: Talk to *them*, you understand.

[TAKA *goes into the house.* ELLEN *sprawls on the steps.* JAMES *and* TOBY *come in from the road.* JAMES *carries* TOBY's *suitcase. He puts them down.*]

JAMES: This is it. And what a lovely view. The homestead . . . and the Reluctant Pupil.

ELLEN: What are you going on about, Jimmy?

JAMES: This is your governess, Mrs Parks.

TOBY: Hello.

JAMES: This is Ellen. She's Marshal's daughter.

ELLEN: Hello. Welcome to Cane Manor.

TOBY: Thank you. I'm sorry to hear you're a Reluctant Pupil.

ELLEN: That's just the Flying Limey's way of being horrible. Still, it's good to see a man doing what he does best.

TOBY: I'm sure we'll work things out. And we'll work well together and, you know, I think it'll . . . work out well. It'll be good. Things will get done.

[ELLEN *smiles perfunctorily.*]

ELLEN: Sure. There'll be lots to do.

JAMES: Ellen has been seen by some as...

ELLEN: Troublesome.

JAMES: Yes, and just a touch moody. Just a touch. In fact, if the truth be known, she's quite difficult.

ELLEN: Talks to herself. Or do I? Yes. Would you like a drink, have a drink?

TOBY: Ah. Yes. Thank you. That would be won-n-derful.

ELLEN: Taka! We need a drink, a drink for Mrs Parks. Can you get a drink?

TAKA: [*from the house*] Okay!

ELLEN: We'll have some kava.

TAKA: Okay!

[ELLEN *squirts out a broken smile at* TOBY.]

ELLEN: I hope you feel welcome.

TOBY: Yes. Thank you.

ELLEN: You live in Sydney?

TOBY: Yes.

ELLEN: What's it like?

TOBY: Oh. You know. Busy. I think it's got its points. There are lots of people, all doing their various things.

JAMES: What about you? Aren't you doing various things?

TOBY: Oh yes. Oh yes. I've got a life there. I've got a life.

ELLEN: But you're here now.

TOBY: Yes. I choose to be here.

ELLEN: What kind of material is that? Your dress.

TOBY: Oh, it's basically cotton. With some kind of synthetic. It's nothing much really. And it's got a bit dirty. I think I'll throw it out.

ELLEN: Is that what's in fashion?

TOBY: Well, yes, but fashion's not just what clothes are in vogue this year. It's a synthesis of the times and what the expectations of the people are.

> [*Pause.* TOBY *realises her half-remembered, half-bohemian coffee shop philosophy is inappropriate in this setting.*]

I'm sorry. That was absolute guff.

JAMES: Come inside and I'll show you your room and you can freshen up and things.

TOBY: Oh. All right. Thanks.

JAMES: The house is just standard Colonial Sugar Refining Company issue, Field Officers for the use of, but it's not bad inside and the verandah is magnificent. It's reasonably cool, which is a pleasant surprise.

> [JAMES *picks up the cases and heads for the verandah as he speaks.* TOBY *follows.* PHILIP *enters from the road.* ELLEN *fails to move her legs to let* JAMES *go up to steps.*]

ELLEN: You've got another customer.

> [TOBY *and* JAMES *turn and regard* PHILIP.]

JAMES: Hello, Philip. This is your new governess.

PHILIP: I guessed that.

TOBY: I think 'governess' is a bit, you know, well . . .

JAMES: Stuffy?

TOBY: Yes, it's a bit too severely Edwardian I think, really. I mean, I've only got a Dip. Ed., you know.

JAMES: Well then, this is Toby Parks, Dip. Ed., your coach and tutor. I hope you'll keep the paper darts to a minimum. This is Philip. He lives nearer Lautoka, where his father's a Field Superintendent, a bara-sahib, one of those ghost-who-walks types.

TOBY: Hello.

[*She shakes hands with the taciturn* PHILIP.]

PHILIP: How do you do.

TOBY: He's a big boy, isn't he? I mean, a grown-up boy. Or really, I mean, he's a young man. Gosh, I'm sorry to talk about you in front of you. Look, I'm sure we'll do lots of hard work and I'm sure we'll enjoy it, too. And we'll get all fixed up as far as exams are concerned.

PHILIP: Sure.

TOBY: He's quiet, isn't he? He's a quiet boy. Which is good, I think.

ELLEN: He's probably sulking.

PHILIP: That'd be right.

ELLEN: He's always sulking. Well, not always. Sometimes . . . when he's not sulking he broods. I'm not being unkind, am I?

PHILIP: No, no.

ELLEN: Philip's a good boy, though. As you say, a good big boy. I love having a go at him because you always get a bite.

JAMES: God save us from Ellen. That's what the natives chant.

ELLEN: [*grinning*] Oh, you shut up. At least I know when I'm being awful.

TOBY: Oh. Well.

[*She looks around for her cases.*]

JAMES: You seem a bit lost.

TOBY: Me? Oh . . . no . . .

JAMES: Don't let these ruffians get you down. If I had my way they'd be sent out to work in the cane fields.

ELLEN: Oh, here we go.

JAMES: I would indeed. They failed their matric. Fine. Send
'em out to earn a living. All this second-chance nonsense
is nonsense.

ELLEN: Bosh, bosh, bosh.

TOBY: But if we knew *why* they failed we'd be in a much
better position to, to —

JAMES: Make sure it . . .

TOBY: Yes, make sure it wouldn't happen again. Wouldn't
we?

   [*There is no response from* ELLEN *or* PHILIP.]

So why — do you think — did you fail? I mean, you
know, in your, your view.

   [*There is still no response from* ELLEN *or* PHILIP.]

Oh dear. I'm sorry. I hardly know you. I shouldn't ask
questions like that.

JAMES: Don't worry about it, don't worry. You wouldn't
know, would you, Ellen? You wouldn't know, anyway.

ELLEN: Wouldn't care, you mean.

JAMES: Hey. Now look. Before you get any ruder. This is a
new regime under Toby and there will not be any cheek
or slacking. Whatever might have gone before is hereby
buried. I hope that's understood.

ELLEN: Sir.

PHILIP: Well, I came here to meet you and I've met you so I
might get on my bike and get going before the storm.
Goodbye.

ELLEN: Philip, why don't you stay and have some kava?
We're going to teach Mrs Parks how to drink kava.

TOBY: I really think it's going to have to be 'Toby'. That
all right with you, Philip? Will you call me Toby?

PHILIP: Of course. I mean, if that's what you want.

TOBY: It is, I think. Ellen?

ELLEN: If you like.

   [TAKA *comes out on to the verandah carrying a large
   bowl of kava and some half-coconut pannikins.*]

TAKA: Kava!

JAMES: Oh God, here we go. The bloody initiation rite.

ELLEN: This is *not* an initiation rite. If Mrs Parks — Toby
— is thirsty, she'll appreciate a drink. If not, she won't.

JAMES: Put it down here, Taka. This is Mrs Parks, by the way. Taka.

TOBY: Hello.

TAKA: *Bula*. Welcome to Fiji.

TOBY: *Vinaka*.

TAKA: That's very good.

JAMES: Bit of a model tourist, aren't you?

TOBY: I enjoy being a model tourist. And I'd love to try some kava.

[TAKA *puts the bowl on the ground in the yard and sits cross-legged next to it.*]

TAKA: You sit here on my right. And the others — as you wish.

[*They sit in a circle around the kava bowl.*]

ELLEN: Now. You have to clap three times before the person drinks it and then indiscriminate applause afterwards. Okay? You first, Jimmy.

[TAKA *hands* JAMES *a cup of kava. The others clap three times.* JAMES *drinks the kava. The others applaud.*]

Now Toby.

[TAKA *hands a cup of kava to* TOBY. *She examines the muddy water uncertainly. The others clap three times.*]

TOBY: You're supposed to drink it all in one go, are you?

ELLEN: Yes. Don't worry. It might look like ditch-water but it tastes quite different.

TOBY: What happens if you don't . . . drink it at all?

ELLEN: Nothing. The sun will still shine. But you will have missed. Somehow you will have missed.

[TOBY *bolts down the kava. The others applaud.* MARSHAL *comes in from the road.*]

MARSHAL: Well look at this. She's gone native already.

[TOBY *stands. The others drink their kava in turn.*]

You're Billy's girl, eh? Billy's niece?

TOBY: Yes.

MARSHAL: Now what is it? Tommy? That right?

TOBY: Toby. Or Elspeth.

MARSHAL:. Oow, dunno about Elspeth. (*Laughing*) You

name it, I'll call you by it.

TOBY: Toby.

MARSHAL: Toby it is. My name's Marshal.

TOBY: I've met your daughter. Oh, and Philip, too.

MARSHAL: Pain in the neck, aren't they? Why they failed I'll never know. Ought to be swabbed by the stewards. Taka! Let's get going with a bit of lunch, shall we?

TAKA: Lunch for everybody?

MARSHAL: Nah. Or wait a minute. Philip, you stay for lunch. You can have your first lesson this afternoon.

TOBY: Oh. I rather thought —

MARSHAL: Doesn't have to be anything special. Just give 'em a team talk and say we're all going to pull together and all that, you know?

TOBY: Sure.

MARSHAL: Now, how about a drink for the horse? Come on, Jim. You've had your fill.

[MARSHAL *converges on the kava. He takes* JAMES's *place in the circle and* JAMES *joins* TOBY.]

JAMES: That's Marshal.

TOBY: Now let me get this straight. Marshal is the what?

JAMES: He's the sahib, the Field Officer.

TOBY: And he's the boss of the area.

JAMES: Not quite. The Field Superintendent is above him. He's the bara-sahib.

TOBY: So *he's* the boss.

JAMES: Not really. Marshal knows this area better than anyone, and they trust him — with good reason — and as it's all sugar cane, he's the effective governor. None of your democracy around here.

TOBY: That I gathered.

JAMES: You're not *seriously* a member of the *Labor* Party, are you?

TOBY: Well, as serious as . . . well, I'm paid up.

JAMES: Good God. May I ask what, why, you . . . ?

TOBY: Oh, I just thought one should have a go. Don't let it ruin your complexion.

JAMES: Oh no. Sorry. I mean you . . . run your life. I was just surprised.

TOBY: Anything else I should know about Marshal?

JAMES: As far as what-have-you's concerned, there's a matron at the hospital in Lautoka, a widow, an 'NZ Lass' as Marshal calls her, although she's fifty or so. They work out okay.

MARSHAL: [*calling out*] Jimmy!

JAMES: Yes, boss.

MARSHAL: You reckon you could have yourself a bit of a wrestle with a pencil and paper and let me know just what exactly you want for the new airfield?

JAMES: You want my plan and detailed proposal?

MARSHAL: Anything that might conceivably look as if you've spent two consecutive minutes on it.

JAMES: Okay, Marshal. See you at lunch, Toby.

TOBY: Oh. Sure.

[JAMES *goes into the house.*]

MARSHAL: Righto. Let's get moving.

[ELLEN, PHILIP, *and* TAKA *go into the house.*]

And how's old Billy going?

TOBY: Oh, he's, you know, medium.

MARSHAL: Old Billy. I wrote to him and said 'Billy, we've got a problem here of an academic nature.' And he wrote back and said, 'Marshal, that's too bloody bad.' But eventually he said, 'My niece — who's inherited my looks — is a highly regarded teacher and coach and she's comparatively new to the game, although' — and here I fail to paraphrase — 'she is a woman of beauty and maturity.'

[MARSHAL *has scooped himself a cup of kava.* TOBY *claps once and then catches herself.*]

MARSHAL: } Don't worry about that now.

TOBY: } Sorry. Just . . .

MARSHAL: So if you weren't always a teacher, what were you?

TOBY: Oh. Well. I was an art student . . . and, well, a bit of a model . . . um . . . and then a telephonist . . . and then I was married . . . a war widow . . . a student again, this time English instead of Art . . . and then a teacher and, as Uncle Billy suggested, a highly regarded tutor. My hobbies include knitting and golf.

MARSHAL: So you're really new to this governess game.

TOBY: Yes, I am. But the young people seem bright and I'm confident that . . .

MARSHAL: Sure, sure. Look. It's all a bit of window-dressing really. You put a bomb under their arse and they'll bolt this exam.

TOBY: Why do you think they failed?

MARSHAL: Oh, I don't know, it's just this . . . adolescent . . . sort of thing, you know. I mean, you take young Ellen. Now I've had to bring her up as best I could — her mother's dead, you know.

TOBY: Yes, yes.

MARSHAL: And well, you know, it's adolescence. I mean, you know, she's got young Philip there on a string and he's a bit, I don't know, sensitive...and it's, well, I think it's all a question of adolescence. Actually I was hoping you might sort it out.

TOBY: Oh. Well. Don't think I'm much of a problem-solver.

MARSHAL: You'll do fine. I can tell that just by looking at you.

TOBY: Teaching's not as easy as it looks.

MARSHAL: Of course not. What I mean is you're very welcome. Have some kava.

TOBY: Thank you.

MARSHAL: Looks like something out of an Arab's canal but it's good, makes your tongue go all fuzzy. It's a kind of narcotic. And a heck of a good drink.

TOBY: It's very nice.

[*They drink.*]

MARSHAL: Now tell me. What's Sydney like these days?

TOBY: It's spreading out. Lots of suburbs. People are settling down.

MARSHAL: Except for you.

TOBY: Except for me. I got out — temporarily at least.

MARSHAL: Yeah, I got out temporarily.

[*He laughs and then stops, looking out to the road.*]
Fiji's not as easy as it looks, either.

[ILLY *comes in from the road. He carries a petrol*

container. He leans against the shed watching them.]

ILLY: Good morning, sahib.

MARSHAL: Hello, Illy. Come on a social call, have you?

ILLY: No, sahib.

MARSHAL: What do you want, Illy? As if I didn't know.

ILLY: [*holding up the container*] The truck belonging to the sirdah of the railway gang has run out of petrol. He asked me to fill this for him.

MARSHAL: That railway gang has never had a more moronic sirdah than that, what's his name?

ILLY: Ram.

MARSHAL: [*turning to* TOBY] Every week you see this happen. Some goose'll run out of petrol and shamble up here with a demi-john and help himself. You'd think you wouldn't have to be in Mensa to read a petrol gauge.

[ILLY *has been studying* TOBY's *form.*]

I suppose you will want me to perform an introduction to this young lady.

ILLY: Thank you, sahib.

MARSHAL: This is Mrs Elspeth Parks and this is Illy.

ILLY: How do you do.

TOBY: Hello.

MARSHAL: Perhaps you'd like to go and freshen up, Toby.

TOBY: All right. Um . . .

[*She fingers the cases.*]

ILLY: I'll take them in for you.

MARSHAL: No! You send Philip out, will you Toby?

TOBY: All right.

ILLY: See you again, Mrs Parks.

TOBY: Yes. Yes.

ILLY: I'll be in Lautoka this afternoon. Perhaps if you'd like to have a look around I could show you some of the cultural highlights of the city.

TOBY: I'm . . . not quite sure what I'm doing. It's all . . . you know . . . up in the air. Thanks, anyway.

[*She goes into the house.*]

ILLY: Where's Mr Parks?

MARSHAL: He was shot down over Italy in 1944.

ILLY: Alas.

MARSHAL: She's a house-guest of mine, Illy, and she's going to be treated by everyone around here as a house-guest of mine.

ILLY: I didn't come here to talk about your house-guest, sahib. And there's no great hurry with the petrol.

MARSHAL: All right, then. What is it, Illy?

[ILLY *pulls out a wad of money and tosses it to* MARSHAL.]

ILLY: It's three hundred pounds.

MARSHAL: Yes.

ILLY: Do you know anyone else around here with three hundred pounds?

MARSHAL: What's your point, Illy?

ILLY: I saw the bara-sahib and he said sugar quotas would be going up.

MARSHAL: Yes, could be.

ILLY: And the marginal lands at the end of the valley would be up for lease.

MARSHAL: Maybe.

ILLY: I'd like to lease twelve acres. As you can see, sahib, I have enough capital for bulls, a plough, fertiliser, everything I'll need.

MARSHAL: So you want to become a cane farmer, Illy?

ILLY: I can do the job.

MARSHAL: Have some kava. Go on.

[ILLY *scoops up some kava.*]

So, Illy. You're forsaking women for property, are you?

ILLY: Only because women are forsaking me for property, sahib.

MARSHAL: Well, you know, Illy, it's all a bit premature.

ILLY: I worked hard to get that three hundred pounds.

MARSHAL: I'm sure you did. But Illy, I wouldn't beat that drum too loudly when a few of us know what you get up to with rich lady visitors.

ILLY: I would classify that as hard work too, sahib.

MARSHAL: By jees you might be right.

ILLY: When will you make the decision?

MARSHAL: [*tossing back the money*] I don't know. For one thing, we don't know if or what cane will grow in the marginal lands.

ILLY: I have selected Ragnar as my cane variety. It will grow there. And it will be a mortgage-lifter. The cane-breeders have proved it.

MARSHAL: Oh yeah. You sound as if you're ready to settle down, Illy.

ILLY: Yes, sahib.

MARSHAL: Well, I'll have to think about it, Illy.

[ILLY *goes over to the petrol bowser and starts filling the container.*]

ILLY: You know what the Hindus say around here. That the Field Officers are *mai/bop* to the farmers. Mother and father.

MARSHAL: I know a bit of Hindi. I studied it for three years.

ILLY: There wouldn't be any favouritism shown towards these 'children', one would hope.

MARSHAL: We'll have to wait and see.

ILLY: Look, Marshal, there's no use putting this off. Let's do our business now.

MARSHAL: No, you look. I'll give you the tom thumb. That land is not mine to give and anyway we don't know how far up sugar quotas are going to go. So don't come round here and try to huckster me off my feet because it won't get you anywhere.

ILLY: I'll come back later, sahib.

MARSHAL: I wouldn't bother, Illy. Not just yet. In any case, the bara-sahib has the final say.

ILLY: I'll come back later. It's no trouble, sahib.

[ILLY *picks up* TOBY's *suitcases.*]

MARSHAL: I'll take those.

[*He takes the cases.*]

ILLY: There's no one else, sahib. No one else with three hundred pounds.

MARSHAL: I take your point, Illy. Goodbye for now.

[*He turns and starts up the steps, then he stops and looks around at* ILLY. ILLY *turns and goes as* MARSHAL *continues up the steps.* PHILIP *appears briskly and takes the cases from* MARSHAL.]

PHILIP: I'll take those in, Marshal.

MARSHAL: Good boy.

> [ELLEN *comes out on to the verandah.*]

ELLEN: But if you *know* that is the direction then *is* that a reason for giving up the journey? Or is it the *journey* itself? Perhaps you know all along what the result will be.

MARSHAL: Ellen.

ELLEN: Yes.

MARSHAL: Give it a rest.

> [PHILIP *goes into the house.* ELLEN *sprawls on the steps.*
>
> Cross fade in on TOBY *walking past the ice cream shop in Lautoka.* ELLEN *and* MARSHAL *go.* ILLY *comes out of the shop with two ice creams.*]

TOBY: Oh, hello.

ILLY: Hello. This is for you.

TOBY: Really?

ILLY: I saw you coming.

TOBY: Oh.

ILLY: And it's a hot day.

TOBY: Yes, it's well and truly freckle time — for me.

ILLY: And I thought you might like to cool down.

TOBY: [*taking the ice cream from him*] Well, thank you. Is this a local custom?

ILLY: No.

TOBY: Well, it's a damn good idea, just the same.

ILLY: It was a pretty good sight, you walking down the street.

TOBY: Oh, it's a won-n-nderful street, a won-n-nderful sight, I liked the smell and colour and, wait a minute, you mean *I* was the sight, the pretty good sight?

ILLY: You and the street and everything, it all goes well together. The colours. . .

TOBY: Oh, I'll say. I love it. I feel so free here. There's no grind. And I *love* the colours. I've just seen this won-n-nderful dress shop. It's got these won-n-nderful mirrors all glimmered around the centre, which is like a boxing ring, and the colours of the material — they're out of the centre of the earth. It's won-n-nderful. All I bought was a top, though. I must go back at some stage.

ILLY: You got off the mark pretty early with your sight-
seeing.

TOBY: Yes. Yes. I just felt like it.

ILLY: You're an intriguing woman, Elspeth.

TOBY: Oh, yes.

ILLY: I mean it. I really do. Why do you say 'oh yes' like
that?

TOBY: Oh, I . . . just meant it — what you said — sounded
like, well it is a bit of a line, isn't it?

ILLY: A line? I don't understand.

TOBY: Well, you know . . . a line . . . a . . . um . . .

ILLY: Please go on. I'm very interested.

TOBY: Well, yes, I bet you are.

ILLY: Please. Don't stop on my account.

TOBY: I didn't stop because I . . .

ILLY: I really am interested, Elspeth.

TOBY: Call me Toby.

ILLY: No, I'll call you Elspeth.

TOBY: All right.

ILLY: I find you intriguing. All I can do is say what I think.
Is there something wrong with my saying that?

TOBY: No. I just thought . . . it's a bit early for that, isn't it?

ILLY: I don't understand. After I've known you for some
years you probably wouldn't be intriguing.

TOBY: No . . . no . . .

ILLY: Absorbing, but not intriguing. It would only be in the
early days that you or I could be intriguing to the other.

TOBY: Early days?

ILLY: Yes.

TOBY: I try not to think about the future.

ILLY: I don't think it's anything to worry about.

TOBY: I still think you're handing me a line.

ILLY: What's a line?

TOBY: A line is . . . it's a mode of behaviour whereby one
person, say X, gets the impression that another person, Y,
wants to . . . um . . . you know . . . have congress?

ILLY: [*smiling broadly*] I see. I see. That's what I thought it
meant.

TOBY: You understand? So I think you're handing me a line.

ILLY: I understand. Would you like another ice cream?

TOBY: Thank you.

> [TOBY *sits on the bench outside the shop.* ILLY *goes into the shop.* TOBY *looks at the sky. And then she smiles. She finds a purse on the bench.* ILLY *comes out with two cups of kava.*]

ILLY: The boys are drinking kava.

TOBY: Well then, we must follow suit.

> [ILLY *gives her a cup. They drink.*]

I found this purse on the bench. Shall I just leave it here?

ILLY: Yes.

> [*She leaves the purse on the bench.*]

TOBY: We didn't *properly* meet, did we?

ILLY: Yes, we did.

TOBY: Yes, you're right. We did. And you work for Marshal?

ILLY: No. I work for myself.

TOBY: But you want to work for Marshal.

ILLY: No, I want to start a cane farm in the marginal lands, the foothills at the end of the valley. There's no cane grown there at present, but I can do it. But I need Marshal's recommendation.

TOBY: Won't he give it to you?

ILLY: I don't know. I've worked hard, I've worked on cane farms, I've been a tourist . . . ah, guide, and now I want to get into those marginal lands. CSR owns them and I want the lease. But they usually only give a piece of the valley to someone who comes from the valley. Someone's son or brother-in-law. Do you know what 'nepotism' means?

TOBY: Yes. Where do you come from?

ILLY: Nowhere in particular.

TOBY: Have you thought of going back to India?

ILLY: *Back* to India? I've never been there. I come from Fiji.

TOBY: Oh.

ILLY: I'm a Fijian Indian.

TOBY: Sorry.

ILLY: It's all right. I suppose I am Indian . . . in a sense . . . one of those people who can work hard in hot weather. Do you know anyone else — apart from us Indians — who works hard in hot weather?

TOBY: None of my students to date. Hello, Ellen.

    [ELLEN *comes on, walking down the street.*]

ELLEN: Hello. Whose purse is that?

TOBY: We don't know. Have you met Illy?

ELLEN: Oh yes. Illy's a frequent visitor to our house.

TOBY: I suppose you're really hammering away at Marshal.

ELLEN: Oh no. It's always when Daddy's out.

ILLY: Social calls . . .

TOBY: Yes. Well. Are you looking forward to your lessons, Ellen?

ELLEN: Can I be frank?

TOBY: Of course. I hope you will.

ELLEN: I'm not looking forward to them at all.

TOBY: Ellen reminds me of what I was like twenty years ago.

ILLY: In what sense?

TOBY: Oh, she's very . . . um . . . ah . . .

ILLY: Forthright?

TOBY: Yes. Forthright.

ELLEN: So would you be if you had to put up with what I have to.

TOBY: I'm sure it'll all pan out, Ellen.

ILLY: Can you picture yourself in twenty years' time?

TOBY: Who, me?

    [*She pauses.*]

  Oh. No.

    [*Shaking her head.*]

  I must get back. Are we all going back?

    [*The others nod.*]

  Then let's go.

    [*She goes out.* ELLEN *starts to follow. She turns and sees* ILLY *pocket the purse.* ILLY *grins.* ELLEN *shakes her head resignedly, then she goes out.* ILLY *follows.*

    Cross fade in on PHILIP *practising his bowling. There are some cricket balls at the foot of the verandah steps.* PHILIP *picks one up and starts his run-up. He bowls, disappearing in the direction of the road, then he comes back for another ball. He runs off and bowls again.*

> TAKA *comes out and puts some drinks on the verandah table and then goes back into the house.* PHILIP *comes back and* MARSHAL *comes in from the road.*]

MARSHAL: Keep it well up. You've got to draw the batsman forward. You bowl short to any good batsman and he'll give you Old Harry.

PHILIP: What happens if he's not a strong player off the back foot?

MARSHAL: Just keep it well up.

> [MARSHAL *approaches the steps.* PHILIP *bowls again.* TOBY *comes out on the verandah.*]

Good evening. That's very smart, that...

TOBY: The top? I bought it in Lautoka. Thank you.

MARSHAL: Had a look around, have you?

TOBY: Well, not as such. I did some shopping.

MARSHAL: I'll show you round the valley tomorrow.

TOBY: Marvellous.

> [PHILIP *comes back.*]

Hello, Philip.

PHILIP: Hello.

> [*He picks up a ball and then runs off and bowls.*]

MARSHAL: Sparkling conversationalist, isn't he? Yes, well, that's the valley down there. And you can just see the sea.

TOBY: Oh yes. Yes. And the cane fields are all down there, are they?

MARSHAL: That's right. All CSR territory. We lease the farms. Looks like a good harvest this year, too.

TOBY: Marvellous. That's when you...what, you cut the...

MARSHAL: We cut the cane, yeah.

TOBY: You cut the cane and. Then. What? You pile it up ...

MARSHAL: We pile it up and —

TOBY: You do pile it up, yes, yes.

MARSHAL: And...we, uh, haul it down to the railway.

TOBY: Ah, those little trucks. And they're pulled by a kind of...what, train-type thing.

MARSHAL: The sugar train, yes.

TOBY: The sugar train. Marvellous. What, and then it's off

to the mill.

MARSHAL: That's right.

TOBY: Uh, har. Yes. Well, it's all, you know, step by step sort of thing. I mean, it looks like hard work.

MARSHAL: It's not easy, round harvest time.

TOBY: Mmm. Mmm.

MARSHAL: But we always get through it.

TOBY: Uh, har.

MARSHAL: Would you like a drink?

TOBY: That would be wonderful. Oh, yes.

MARSHAL: What would you like?

TOBY: Whisky and soda with ice, please.

[MARSHAL *pours her a drink.*]

MARSHAL: You like a drop, do you?

TOBY: Oh...you know, yes. These are all small farms, are they?

MARSHAL: Yeah. It's a funny system, when you look at it with any degree of objectivity. It's part peasant agriculture, part big plantation, a mixture of incentives and volume. You look down this valley and across to the coast, you'll see a hundred aspirations, a whole network of carrots and sticks, about four generations of Indians beavering away and it all works. CSR shipped ninety-nine thousand tons of sugar out of Fiji last year.

TOBY: Are they all Indians down there?

MARSHAL: Just about. The Fijians won't work in the cane fields. They will not touch it. They will not bend their backs to pick up a sixpence. That's why the Indians were brought over here in the first place. The Fijians are too busy fishing and drinking kava and politicking and what have you to cut any cane.

TOBY: Politicking?

MARSHAL: Oh yes. They'll get over the top of the Indians and the whites, you wait and see.

TOBY: That, um, Indian? The one called Illy?

MARSHAL: Oh, yes.

TOBY: You don't think that he would succeed or, you know, do anything?

MARSHAL: I'm not too sure about Illy. On any count. But

don't misconstrue what I am, ah, expounding. The Indians have got commerce and so on by the throat. But the Fijians know what it's all about when it comes to politics. I'd say all in all it's pretty well balanced.

TOBY: I met Illy in Lautoka this afternoon.

MARSHAL: Oh, yes.

TOBY: He just bumped into me.

MARSHAL: Oh, yes.

TOBY: He seems to have a lot of go in him.

MARSHAL: Yes.

TOBY: I think it's wonderful here. I think it's wonderful that you're producing something. So much of life is unproductive.

MARSHAL: Yeah. But it's only sugar. Still, it's on every table in the world.

[TAKA *comes out with a bowl of fruit.*]

TAKA: Hello. *Bula.* Good evening.

MARSHAL: Here she is. And how's Taka this evening?

TAKA: Well, thank you, *turanga.* There was a boy from Mr Ram's up here this afternoon.

MARSHAL: What, old Ram, on the Nadi road?

TAKA: Yes.

MARSHAL: [*to* TOBY] We've got more Rams around here than a sheep station.

TAKA: The boy wanted a flood gate.

MARSHAL: CSR does not provide flood gates on private farms. Short answer for Mr Ram.

TAKA: The boy said he would come back for an answer tomorrow evening.

MARSHAL: I'll go down and see the old man tomorrow morning. He's got to hand the land over to his son. The silly old goat — had two sons, and shipped the bright one off to university in Madras. The slow one's being groomed — for what seems like a century — to take over the farm. Should have been the other way round, and I told him so. Not that I am in any way opposed to higher learning or the fruits thereof.

TOBY: I'm pleased to hear that.

MARSHAL: It is indeed a wondrous thing. So what have you

been up to, Taka? Been hiding from Illy, have you?

TAKA: Well no, you see, I am going to a dance in Sigatoka and I am going with someone else and Illy says he is very angry, so I say to him, 'Look, I am not your personal property and in any case Apisai has asked me and he is very nice.'

MARSHAL: And he's got a car.

TAKA: That is absolutely right.

[MARSHAL *and* TAKA *laugh.* TOBY *wanders thoughtfully over to the drinks.*]

MARSHAL: You reckon you'll ever go out in public with Illy?

TAKA: If I feel like it.

[*Pause.*]

And if he ever gets a car.

[MARSHAL *and* TAKA *laugh.* TOBY *is not impressed.* PHILIP *comes back and drops the cricket balls. He keeps one and prepares to bowl.*]

MARSHAL: Ohr, you're not gunna bowl any more, are you? Come on, pack it in. Get yourself a beer, go on.

[PHILIP *goes over towards the drinks.* TAKA *motions him to stop. She hands him a beer.*]

Well, I hope you can make something of him, Toby. BHP don't take morons. They can have their pick of the cream of the crop. You've got to be looking at two first-class honours and four As to be taken on as a BHP cadet.

PHILIP: I'm not sure I want to be a BHP cadet.

MARSHAL: Not sure? You should be bloody glad anyone'll take you on. And if BHP does, well that's the tops.

PHILIP: Maybe.

MARSHAL: After CSR, of course. But Duckknuckles here doesn't want to take after his father.

[PHILIP *wanders up on to the verandah, polishing a cricket ball.*]

What gets into these young fellers? I suppose you've got something inside you, you've got to work it out, you've got to get rid of it and then you become an adult. Ah well, too bloody bad. I've got my work cut out getting a daughter off my hands.

[JAMES *and* ELLEN *come out on the verandah.*]

Anyway, time to say a few words of welcome. Ladies and gentlemen.

JAMES: Speech, speech.

MARSHAL: Your prayers have been answered, cully, for that is precisely what I am upstanding for. Toby, as we've come to know you in the short time you've been here, it's good to see you, *bula*, welcome to Fiji, and let's all look forward to making your acquaintance on a basis of a more detailed nature. Now it's time for the address-in-reply from the guest-of-honour and then we'll all get stuck into the turps.

[*There is general laughter and applause.* ILLY *comes in from the road.* TOBY *was well brought up, and she does this just right.*]

TOBY: Thank you, Marshal. And I'd like to thank all of you for coming. I've got to like Fiji a lot, even though I haven't seen much of the night life yet, this being my first day. I'd especially like to say to my students, Philip and Ellen, thank you for your welcome, and if I could borrow from Marshal's inimitable exhortation, let's all get stuck into the work. Thank you all for coming and being so friendly and, lastly, *bula* and *vinaka*.

[*They all applaud.* MARSHAL *busies himself with drinks.* ILLY *approaches* TAKA. *She goes into the house, then he approaches* TOBY.]

ILLY: That was very good.

TOBY: You were intrigued?

ILLY: I just thought you spoke very well.

[JAMES *approaches.*]

JAMES: Indeed she did. That was a wonderful speech. Very articulate.

TOBY: Oh. Gosh. Thanks.

JAMES: I think she even got the accent right on *bula* and . . .

ILLY: *Vinaka*. Yes, she did.

TOBY: What *praise* I get.

JAMES: I know you'll be busy with your call to arms and hard work, but if you've got time and you want to see a bit more I could take you up in the Moth so you can see Mana Island and the coral and all that.

TOBY: Mmmm. Thank you.

JAMES: It's worth seeing, isn't it Illy?

ILLY: Yes.

JAMES: Or. I could rent a Sunderland. We could land in the sea near Mana and go ashore. Or swim ashore. It really is, to coin a phrase, a tropical paradise.

TOBY: Oh, really.

ILLY: You've got a big ... there ... just hold still.

[TOBY *is still.* ILLY *runs his finger down her temple and then removes something. He brushes her face with his hand.*]

A slow mosquito. But don't worry. We don't have malaria here. Just a few million bugs.

TOBY: Gosh.

ILLY: I've got to see Taka about something. Excuse me.

[ILLY *goes into the house.*]

JAMES: Interesting chap, isn't he?

TOBY: Yes.

[TOBY *reflects for a moment and then wanders over and picks up a bottle of beer.*]

Would you like a beer, Ellen?

ELLEN: Erk no.

MARSHAL: Those manners aren't too crash-hot.

ELLEN: Erk, no thanks.

TOBY: Here, Marshal. You carry the torch. I must go in and clean up before dinner. Excuse me.

JAMES: Sure. *Bula.*

[TOBY *hands the bottle to* MARSHAL. *She goes into the house.* MARSHAL *comes over and tops up* JAMES's *drink.*]

How do you think she'll go, Marshal?

MARSHAL: I reckon. That she will be a beauty. A beauty.

JAMES: One wonders if there's not a bit of tizziness there. Do you think she's tizzy?

MARSHAL: I think she will be a beauty.

JAMES: Yes. Yes. It's endearing, of course. I mean, I'm endeared, for one.

MARSHAL: You might have a bit of competition.

JAMES: Not Illy again?

[MARSHAL *nods.*]

How boring. And it's not as if, you know, you get the impression that he's enjoying himself all that much. Although I suppose he must.

MARSHAL: He enjoys himself.

JAMES: Yes, he must. Well, it's impossible not to, really, when you come down to it. I intend to, in this case.

MARSHAL: Have you got that plan for the airfield?

JAMES: Not yet. It's just this bloody . . . lassitude. You sit down, you think, oh, I don't know. I'm sorry. Tomorrow. Or soon. I mean, you know, it's just . . . you've just got to sit down and bang bang bang finish. That's all there is to it. By the way, I thought a hotel near the airstrip would be a good thing.

MARSHAL: There's only a limited amount of marginal land. And if head office says sugar then it's sugar.

JAMES: I'll convince you otherwise. And head office.

[ILLY *comes out on to the verandah.* JAMES *drains his glass.*]

See you at dinner.

[JAMES *goes into the house.*]

ILLY: How are you, Ellen?

ELLEN: Hot and bothered.

ILLY: That's no good. Are you running a temperature?

ELLEN: Not sure.

ILLY: [*feeling her forehead*] No. You'll be all right. A bit of bucking up I think would be in order.

[*She smiles at him.*]

ELLEN: Okay.

[ILLY *approaches* MARSHAL *deferentially and with great reluctance.*]

ILLY: Is there . . . uh . . . anything . . . you want done around the place, sahib?

MARSHAL: No, Illy.

ILLY: Good.

[*He moves off.*]

MARSHAL: Illy.

ILLY: Yes, sahib.

MARSHAL: Not so much of this popping in and out of my

front door sort of routine, eh? There's a good chap.

[ILLY *digests this.*]

ILLY: Yes, sahib.

[ILLY *goes.* PHILIP *picks up a cricket ball.* MARSHAL *goes up the steps.*]

MARSHAL: Get ready for dinner. And see if you can actually help with something.

ELLEN: Yes, Dad.

[MARSHAL *goes into the house.* PHILIP *bowls a ball. He comes back to pick up another one.* ELLEN *sprawls across the steps.*]

Keep practising, Philip. You'll make it to England. If you pay your own fare.

[PHILIP *runs off to bowl another ball. Fade out except on* ELLEN. *She opens a book and reads, then she moves over and sits down on the verandah, still reading. Fade up around* ELLEN. *She and* TAKA *are sitting on the verandah listening to* TOBY *give a lesson late in the afternoon, three weeks later.* TOBY *wears a skirt that matches the top she bought in Lautoka.*]

TOBY: There are two views about the ending of *Great Expectations*. In the first version Pip managed to free himself of his inane love for Estella and returned to London free of all illusions and in full possession of himself.

[ILLY *enters from the road. He wears dusty cricket whites.* TOBY *stops, looks around, and gives* ILLY *a frosty glance. He smilingly waves her on.*]

That was the original ending of the book. The second version, suggested by Bulwer Lytton, ended with Pip and Estella alone on the ruins of Satis House.

[TOBY *looks around.* ILLY *is watching her. She resumes her lesson.*]

The last sentence of the book, which is . . . what is the last sentence of the book, Ellen?

ELLEN: I don't know, ma'am.

TOBY: 'I saw no shadow of another parting from her'. So they get together, the tormentor and the tormented, and one gets the impression of a conventional happy ending grafted on to a novel which already contained an unconventional happy ending on its own terms. Okay?

ELLEN: So the second ending has less social comment.

TOBY: Ellen dear, let's not use terms like 'social comment', shall we? Please.

ELLEN: Why not?

TOBY: Because it's a philistine cliché devised by crib writers and I don't like it. Okay?

ELLEN: Okay.

[TOBY *smiles.*]

TOBY: Right. That's it for today. You can show Philip the work he's missed.

ELLEN: Do I have to?

TOBY: Ellen, dear, please co-operate. Please don't be difficult.

ELLEN: All right.

TAKA: I must go down to Mr Ram's and then report back to Marshal. Come on, Ellen.

ELLEN: What?

TAKA: Come for the walk.

ELLEN: I don't feel like a walk.

TAKA: Come on. Pretty soon you'll be going away all grown up and you won't see me any more.

ELLEN: I won't be doing any of that.

TAKA: Yes you will. Come on.

[ELLEN *hesitates.*]

TOBY: Go on, Ellen.

[TAKA *leads* ELLEN *out.* TOBY *stacks up her books.*]
Did you enjoy the lesson?

ILLY: I wasn't listening.

TOBY: Oh?

ILLY: I was looking at you.

TOBY: Not Taka?

ILLY: Now I understand why you're being so cool. Someone has been talking to you about me.

TOBY: Several people, actually.

ILLY: What do they say?

TOBY: I really don't want to talk about it or get involved in any argument. Now you must be hot. Would you like a drink?

ILLY: No. Tell me one thing. And then I'll drop it.

TOBY: All right. I heard Marshal telling Jimmy that, quote, 'Illy's been through half the female population of Fiji and that was on a bank holiday.'

ILLY: It's an exaggeration.

TOBY: Oh yes?

ILLY: You mean you would judge me on what others say?

TOBY: No.

    [*Pause.*]

I understand you relieved Ellen of her virginity.

ILLY: It was her idea.

TOBY: Apparently after you'd worked her over she was in no mood to find Philip — poor, awkward Philip — a goer.

ILLY: At least I didn't get her pregnant.

TOBY: That's a pretty callous attitude.

ILLY: My neck was on the block, not hers. And she knew that.

TOBY: Did Marshal ever find out?

ILLY: No. That's why I'm still alive. How did you find out?

TOBY: I guessed. That day in the street in Lautoka.

ILLY: Will you keep quiet about it?

TOBY: Of course. What would Marshal do?

ILLY: I don't know. Probably not much more than he's doing now.

TOBY: What's he doing to you?

ILLY: He keeps putting off my request to build a farm in the marginal lands. In the meantime, I'm the only one with the capital and that must prevail, even with Marshal. But if the Ellen business gets out . . .

TOBY: You think you'd be run out of town or something?

ILLY: Well, look at the way you reacted.

TOBY: Oh, I'm just a sook. I don't know why I got so indignant — I've been in and out of hot water myself, over the years.

ILLY: Don't worry about it. Even without that, I haven't been able to get an answer out of Marshal in three weeks.

TOBY: Well, I think that's awful and it's not fair because because you know you've worked hard and you're the logical, the logical one, from what I can see. And you should have the land. And I'm going to tell Marshal that.

ILLY: Thank you. I appreciate that.

[MARSHAL *comes in. He wears cricket whites and red socks.*]

TOBY: Oh hello, Marshal.

[TOBY *hesitates, quails a bit, then resumes stacking up her books.*]

MARSHAL: What's this? You got a new student?

TOBY: Oh, no, he's just an observer. How did the cricket go?

MARSHAL: Not too smoothly. It was CSR versus the Nadi Nondescripts and the Nondescripts got up. And young Philip is none too pleased about it. None too pleased.

TOBY: What happened?

MARSHAL: Ohr, a few of us old fellows dropped a few catches off his bowling. And he was ropable. Couldn't see the funny side of it at all.

TOBY: Oh, well, he's a very intense boy.

MARSHAL: First time you've beaten CSR. That right, Illy?

ILLY: Yes, sahib.

MARSHAL: Illy was one of the stars for the Nondies. Got dropped a few times, though.

ILLY: I took a few selective risks.

MARSHAL: Yeah, hit the ball in my direction.

[MARSHAL *and* ILLY *laugh.* PHILIP *comes in from the road.*]

TOBY: Philip! I hear you bowled very well.

PHILIP: (*sulky*) Three for eighty-five.

TOBY: So you took three wickets. That's very good.

MARSHAL: Hit the stumps all three times.

TOBY: That's very good.

PHILIP: I should have taken seven wickets.

TOBY: Oh, well. You know. So should we all. Now come and get your notes from today. We finished the lesson but you should be able to catch up.

[*She puts her arm around him and leads him over to the table on the verandah.*]

We did *Great Expectations* today. Now you've read it, haven't you?

PHILIP: No.

TOBY: That's very disappointing, Philip. Now come on, I want you to do well, and you can do well. You're a bright boy and it's very silly not to do your best work. Now you tell me why it is that you've got this negative attitude.

PHILIP: I don't know.

[TOBY *looks at him searchingly.*]

ILLY: Have you made up your mind, sahib?

MARSHAL: Yes, I have, Illy. Yes I have. I'm sorry, old son, but I'm afraid I'm going to have to turn you down.

ILLY: [*angrily*] What?

[TOBY *and* PHILIP *turn and watch.*]

MARSHAL: I'd advise you to cop it sweet, Illy. I've decided to put that land to another use or uses. My advice to you is go to Suva with your capital and set yourself up in business. This is a small community here, a closed community. You wouldn't have lasted. You wouldn't have liked it.

ILLY: I would have liked it very much.

MARSHAL: Well, that's as may be. I've made my decision. I'm sorry, Illy.

ILLY: You will think again.

[*He goes off angrily.*]

TOBY: Philip, be a dear boy and bring the kava out, will you? It'll need some stirring, too. You'll find it in the laundry.

[PHILIP *goes inside.*]

Now, Marshal, you come and sit down on the verandah and talk to me.

MARSHAL: My pleasure. But I do have to check a few things in the office first.

TOBY: They can wait. You just come and sit yourself down here.

MARSHAL: All right. Jees, I could do with it after a day of chasing leather. Know any good yarns?

[*He sits down on the verandah.*]

TOBY: Marshal, do you think it's fair that Illy should miss out on that marginal land?

MARSHAL: Look, Toby, you've only just got here, you don't

understand what the whole set-up is, and I don't blame
you — I didn't cotton on to what was happening when I
first came here.

TOBY: Now now just hold on, Marshal, just hold on. I didn't
fight in the War but I think the whole thing was a damn
shame and if I said so you wouldn't disagree.

MARSHAL: Damn shame for some.

TOBY: Now hear me out. Illy's got . . . every right to that
land. Every right. And I don't care how long I've been
here.

MARSHAL: Now look, Toby. For one thing, there are vast
differences — of a religious character — between Illy and
the Hindus around here.

TOBY: I know that, Marshal. I know *all* about the religious
differences.

MARSHAL: Well let's have a drink on it, then.

[MARSHAL *looks around.* TOBY *restrains him.*]

TOBY: I will indeed. But don't you think you can fob me off.

MARSHAL: Now just you hold on. You can tell me *all* the
facts you want, but I know this: Illy is a rogue elephant
and all he's gunna do in this valley is cause trouble. The
people around here are Northern Indians, they're
Hindus, they work hard, they go to the temple and their
children take over when they're grown up and so on. But
Illy? He's wrong. He's wrong all over. He's a Muslim,
nominally, he's a southern Indian, nominally, *and* he's
got a touch of the tar. That's right. His mother was part
Fijian, part Swedish, don't ask me why.

TOBY: Well, you know, Marshal, I wouldn't have picked
that with the naked eye, and I don't see —

MARSHAL: Now, now. Just, just hang on. Just hang on. I
didn't say that he couldn't have the marginal land
because he may or may not have relatives in Stockholm.
That was not my point. I just said I've assessed the
situation from all angles and there are a *number*, a
number of reasons why Illy is *not* the top candidate for
this particular job. There are a *number* of reasons.

[PHILIP *brings out a bowl of kava.* MARSHAL *scoops
some out for* TOBY.]

TOBY: Well, I think it's a big fix and a disgrace and you're going to find me snapping about your ankles for some time to come.

MARSHAL: Well then, so be it. But you get enough kava in you and you'll find your tongue's too thick to do any snapping.

TOBY: Well, I just might try to bring off the double so keep your boots on.

MARSHAL: [*laughing*] Good on you, Toby. You're lucky to have a governess like this, Philip. You could have drawn a real old boiler. Don't you reckon you're lucky?

PHILIP: Yes.

TOBY: Oh, Philip. [*Hugging him*] You've really been put on the spot, haven't you?

PHILIP: I'd reckon.

[*He smiles at her.*]

TOBY: Oh look, a smile. Isn't that wonderful?

[JAMES *comes in, wearing a blazer over cricket whites.*]

JAMES: Hello. Hello. Hello, Philip. Bad luck, old chap.

PHILIP: Next time I'll place my own field.

MARSHAL: That's the spirit. Come and I'll give you one of my Cardus books, as a gesture of atonement.

[*He takes* PHILIP *inside.* JAMES *scoops up some kava.*]

TOBY: How did you go at the cricket?

JAMES: A streaky nineteen. Did you have a good day?

TOBY: Yes, I did. I love it here. I don't know if I'll be able to go back home.

JAMES: You'll start missing it soon.

TOBY: I don't think so. I had a good life in Sydney. But it's all played out.

JAMES: You're not serious.

TOBY: Yes, I am. I don't want to go home-home either. Home-home for me is a small town among the vineyards in the Barossa Valley — and people who drop in with a bottle of beer just to have a look at me when I go back. The best part is when they say 'Just dropped in to have a look at you, Parksy.' Now that is altogether too frank for me in these years of my sunset.

JAMES: But if you stay here, what will you do? What will

you become?

TOBY: I don't know.

JAMES: You must have some idea.

TOBY: Well I'll tell you what I won't do and that's take over that dress shop in Lautoka. I thought briefly about it, but the chances were fairly strong I'd end up as a fairly scatty dress shop lady, the sort of dress shop lady you see with a violet shawl and nicotine stains.

JAMES: And big earrings.

TOBY: Cocker spaniel earrings. The sort of dress shop lady who chatters along, fairly inanely, you'd have to say, and that's being kind, about who's in town and doing what to whom. I would not like to end me days like such a lady, a crone before her time.

JAMES: We'll have to keep you out of the dress shops then.

TOBY: Please do.

JAMES: Come out to dinner with me tonight. We'll go to the Mocambo. You'll soon feel better.

TOBY: Could we make it tomorrow night? I'm feeling a bit tired and there's a chance I could turn morbid.

JAMES: No one marinates seaweed like the chef at the Mocambo. You want to go native, well that's the place. Think about it while I clean up.

TAKA: [*coming in from the road*] Turanga! *Turanga!*

[MARSHAL *comes out of the house, followed by* PHILIP.]

MARSHAL: Yes, Taka, what's the problem?

TAKA: It's Mr Ram.

MARSHAL: On the Nadi road?

TAKA: Yes and his crops are being flooded. The drain at the back is not working the way Mr Ram would like it to work.

MARSHAL: Of course. Mr Ram. It's nearly dinner time. I get nothing but trouble from that old goat, especially around meal times. It's a case of ripening senility.

JAMES: I'll handle it, Marshal. You go and eat.

MARSHAL: You know where the pump is?

JAMES: Indeed I do. A field officer's shed is a wondrous thing.

[JAMES *opens the shed.*]

Come on, Philip. Give me a hand.

[PHILIP *helps him carry out a pump.*]

MARSHAL: Sure you'll be all right?

JAMES: Go and eat.

MARSHAL: Righto.

[MARSHAL *goes inside.* JAMES *and* PHILIP *make for the road with the pump.*]

TOBY: Jimmy!

JAMES: Yes?

TOBY: What about the Mocambo?

JAMES: It can wait till tomorrow night. As you said.

[*As* JAMES *and* PHILIP *go down the road,* TOBY *remains standing on the verandah.* ILLY *comes back.*]

ILLY: I forgot to say goodbye to you.

TOBY: I'm glad you remembered.

ILLY: Why?

TOBY: I was feeling lonely.

ILLY: It's a pity that I'm not generally welcome around here. I could see a lot more of you.

TOBY: Don't give up hope. I've started to work on Marshal and I'm sure he'll come round.

ILLY: Thanks, but I doubt it. Marshal doesn't like me because he can't control me.

TOBY: Oh come now, Illy. He's not some evil dictator.

ILLY: No. He's very reasonable. But you can't cross him. You can't be independent of him. It's against his principles.

TOBY: Oh, rubbish.

ILLY: He sees himself as the benevolent god of the valley. He gives and all is well. But I don't want his benevolence and he can't stand that.

TOBY: You're damn lucky to have a man like him in charge.

ILLY: I'm not. The others are. That's what they want. But it's not what I want.

TOBY: Don't you think you're carrying this 'loner' business too far, Illy? I mean, you know, we all have to accept some god, benevolent or otherwise. We all have to have some kind of authority, some kind of, well, no we don't really, do we?

ILLY: No.

TOBY: You're absolutely right.

    [ILLY *laughs.* TOBY *laughs too.*]

ILLY: I love you.

TOBY: Whoops a daisy.

    [ILLY *kisses her. She responds, then breaks away.*]
    Gosh. I don't know about this.

ILLY: Yes you do.

    [*They kiss.* ILLY *loosens her top.*]

ILLY: I always said this was a nice top.

TOBY: It wouldn't suit you.

ILLY: [*grinning*] Don't you mock me.

    [*He embraces her.*]

TOBY: Um ... Do you think this is wise?

ILLY: No.

    [*Fade out.*]

END OF ACT ONE

ACT TWO

It is two weeks later, late on a sunny morning. Washing is strung up everywhere.

From behind the washing TOBY *and* ELLEN *can be heard conducting a lesson on the verandah.*

TAKA *takes down the washing and the lines so that the verandah can eventually be seen.*

ELLEN: [*reading badly*] 'This, um, land of, ah, such dear, um . . .'

TOBY: It's not 'This um land of ah such dear um'. It's [*reading well*],

'This land of such dear souls, this dear, dear land,
Dear for her reputation throughout the world
Is now leased out, I die pronouncing it
Like to a tenement, or pelting farm.'

All right?

ELLEN: What does 'pelting farm' mean?

TOBY: Little farm, paltry farm, small-scale farm. Now what does the passage mean?

ELLEN: Um . . . ah . . .

TOBY: What — in your own words — is the substance of your preparation for today?

ELLEN: Nothing.

[*Pause.*]

TOBY: Ellen.

ELLEN: Yes?

TOBY: You can't stay here in Fiji and be seventeen for ever. Pretty soon you'll be eighteen and then twenty-one and even worse than that. And your home won't last, either. One day, not too far off now, your father will retire; and Fiji will stop being a colony; and the Fijians and the Indians will have growing pains of their own. They certainly won't look too kindly on those who are white, unco-operative, and eternally seventeen.

ELLEN: Yeah, well you left the mainland. And Dad. And Jimmy.

125

TOBY: We have all done our time there. And so will you. And in my opinion you'll do better than any of us.

ELLEN: Yes?

TOBY: Yes. The old place will never be the same again. Now. Before you make plans to take life by storm, let's get back to our schoolwork. All right?

[ELLEN *smiles hesitantly.*]

ELLEN: All right.

TOBY: Now. What does the passage mean to you?

ELLEN: He's saying that . . . um . . . this is when you need time, time to . . . um . . . don't get a flash of the future . . . train down . . .

TOBY: What?

ELLEN: Oh. Just talking to myself.

TOBY: Well don't.

ELLEN: What?

TOBY: Don't talk to yourself.

ELLEN: Why not?

TOBY: Because it's silly.

ELLEN: Oh.

TOBY: And I won't have it in my class.

ELLEN: All right.

TOBY: Understand?

ELLEN: Yes.

TOBY: Now what does the passage mean?

ELLEN: It means that the country has been divided and threatens to disintegrate into a series of small estates.

TOBY: That will do me just fine.

[ELLEN *smiles.* TAKA *has cleared the washing away by now and is folding it.*]

But you write in 'pelting farm' and its meaning just the same.

[ELLEN *writes in her book.* PHILIP *enters from the road.*]

Good morning, Philip.

PHILIP: I'm sorry I'm late. My father wanted me to help him deliver some letters to the farmers and Field Officers. So I'm sorry I'm late.

[TOBY *considers him.*]

TOBY: I don't care *what* your father says or *what* he wants
you for. You tell him that I do not start my classes late for
anyone and if you can't be here on time then it's *outski* for
you. Do you understand?

PHILIP: Yes, Mrs Parks.

TOBY: Good. Now you can copy out Ellen's notes.

PHILIP: Yes, Mrs Parks.

[ILLY *comes into the yard, shirtless and carrying a
scythe.* TAKA, TOBY, ELLEN *and* PHILIP *watch him go
over to the shed.*]

TOBY: And then it will be time for lunch.

[ELLEN *shows* PHILIP *her exercise book.* TOBY *sits on
the verandah railing and lights a cigarette.* TAKA *goes
on folding the washing.* ILLY *brings out a sharpening
wheel. He smiles at* TOBY, *who gives him a small,
intimate, confident wave.*]

TAKA: [*brightly*] Hello, Illy.

ILLY: Hello, Taka.

[TOBY *cautiously examines* TAKA, *who goes on folding
up washing.* ILLY *sharpens his scythe on the wheel,
then he stops.*]

Is this interrupting your lesson?

TOBY: Philip. Is that noise disturbing you?

PHILIP: No, Mrs Parks.

TOBY: Taka?

TAKA: Doesn't worry me.

TOBY: Nothing ever does. [*To* ILLY] We're right, thanks.

ILLY: I won't be long.

[ILLY *resumes sharpening the scythe.* PHILIP *continues
writing the passages pointed out by* ELLEN. JAMES
comes out of the house. He has a hangover.]

JAMES: What the hell's that racket?

ILLY: Nearly finished.

JAMES: Hey! You!

[ILLY *finishes.*]

ILLY: All finished.

JAMES: What do you mean by coming around here and
making such a racket?

ILLY: It's my job.

TOBY: Illy's on the railway gang.

> [JAMES *stares at her.*]

  He clears the tracks.

JAMES: Oh yeah? What else is he here for?

TAKA: Illy. You've finished, haven't you?

ILLY: Yes.

TAKA: We're going to have lunch now.

ILLY: Oh yes?

TAKA: And you can come and help me peel some potatoes.

ILLY: I've got to go. Goodbye.

> [ILLY *goes.* JAMES *looks around.*]

JAMES: Look at this mess. Look at it! What the hell's the shed
  for?

> [JAMES *picks up the hoe, the shovel and other pieces of
> equipment and stows them in the shed while the others
> watch. He then slams the door of the shed.*]

TOBY: Did you have a few drinks last night?

JAMES: Yes. Marshal and I got stuck into the turps. What of
  it?

TOBY: Nothing.

JAMES: It's about all you can do in a place like this.

TOBY: Oh, I don't know about that. I love it here. The air in
  the hills is so fresh and sweet I could breathe it for ever. I
  feel so beautifully balanced and inner-sprung. This is
  surely my peak.

JAMES: Oh well, that's wonderful.

> [*He pours himself a glass of water and slumps in a
> chair.*]

ELLEN: Are you serious, Toby?

TOBY: Yes I am.

ELLEN: I'd never thought of this place being like that. You
  seem to be —

PHILIP: Toby, can I ask —

TOBY: Just a minute, Philip. Let Ellen speak.

PHILIP: I want to speak, too.

TOBY: In a minute, Philip dear.

PHILIP: Why does she get to have a go before me?

> [TOBY *puts a playful headlock on* PHILIP *and hugs
> him.*]

TOBY: Oh you be quiet. You're like a schoolboy dividing up a brick of ice cream.

[PHILIP *is more than mollified by this treatment.*]

Now, Ellen.

ELLEN: I was just going to say that you seem to be happy and you seem to be happy in the place you're in.

TOBY: Well, who wouldn't be happy with two wonderful children to look after.

[*She hugs them both.*]

Now. Inside and get ready for lunch and then we resume at two.

PHILIP: I just want to —

ELLEN: Oh, come on, Philip.

[ELLEN *drags* PHILIP *inside.*]

TAKA: Lunch for you two?

TOBY: Yes, please.

JAMES: No, thanks.

TAKA: Orange juice?

JAMES: Yes, please.

[TAKA *goes inside.*]

They're a bit old to be called children, aren't they?

TOBY: Oh, they're not. They've still got a few weeks left before adulthood. And I think they're enjoying their last fling at being children. They're a bit reluctant to grow up and go to the mainland, but who wouldn't be? They'd rather stay on here in a kind of endless morning. But with the help of their doughty governess, they're learning that all good things come to an end. That there is in fact an afternoon.

JAMES: This 'doughty governess' seems to be everything from a mother to a priest.

TOBY: Oh, gosh, no.

[ILLY *comes in from the road and takes the scythe into the shed.* TOBY *watches him.*]

JAMES: Toby.

TOBY: Mmmm?

JAMES: You're a white woman.

TOBY: A freckled woman.

JAMES: An Australian. And you're having a secret affair

with an Indian. Not much of a precedent, is it? You wouldn't want every teacher to follow suit.

TOBY: How did you get into a position whereby you know so much about people's lives?

JAMES: I know. I know. And if everyone gets to know you'll be finished in Fiji.

TOBY: Thank you for the prediction.

JAMES: Look. The skin on my nose isn't affected. I'm just telling you the facts. There's no censure. Just the facts.

TOBY: Oh, sure.

JAMES: Now come on. Don't get all huffy.

[ILLY *emerges from the shed.*]

Illy, perhaps you can sort this out.

ILLY: What?

JAMES: Toby here claims I insulted her.

[TOBY *looks uneasy.*]

ILLY: Oh?

JAMES: Yes indeed. Will you defend her honour?

ILLY: Well, I . . .

JAMES: You'll give it a go. Good. Well this is what happened. She claims that I accused her of cheating at golf.

[ILLY *smiles with involuntary relief.* TOBY *turns and stares at* JAMES.]

ILLY: What did she do?

JAMES: I hesitate to involve you in this.

ILLY: Come on.

JAMES: She substituted one ball for another.

ILLY: Really? Did you do that, Toby?

TOBY: No.

JAMES: Well, there you go. It's an impasse. But I'll tell you what I'll do. I'll withdraw the accusation unconditionally. And I won't ever mention it again. Just to show you what a fine sportsman I am.

ILLY: There you are, Toby. Nothing to worry about.

[ILLY *grins at* TOBY. *She smiles uneasily.*]

JAMES: Unfortunately, though, there is one fly in the ointment. Not everyone is as fine a sportsman as I am and there could be rocky days ahead.

[ILLY's *grin fades.* TOBY *sits down.*

MARSHAL *enters sheepishly, carrying a petrol container.*]

Ay Marshal! Looking for some orange juice?

MARSHAL: Yes, mate.

[JAMES *laughs.*]

JAMES: I'll see you at lunch.

[JAMES *goes into the house.* ILLY *is looking steadily and quizzically at* MARSHAL.]

ILLY: Good afternoon, sahib.

MARSHAL: Ohr yeah, g'day, Illy. How are you popping up, all right?

[MARSHAL *makes his way with no great eagerness towards the petrol bowser.*]

ILLY: I'm well, thank you, sahib.

MARSHAL: Ohr, that's good, Illy. That's good. Working on the gang, are you? Making a bit of money, eh?

ILLY: Enough so that I don't have to dip into my three hundred pounds.

MARSHAL: Oh, yeah. Yeah. That's right, you've got three hundred pounds. That's right.

ILLY: Yes, sahib.

MARSHAL: It's a wonder you don't get into the duty-free caper with that three hundred pounds. You could buy into a shop in Nadi, sell a few watches, mend a few sapphires. You'd be a good salesman, Illy. You'd make real headway among the blue rinse set.

ILLY: I'm happy where I am, sahib. And I think you will find that very few imperfect sapphires are sold by the merchants of Nadi.

MARSHAL: Of course. It was a cheap shot.

ILLY: How have you been getting on, sahib?

MARSHAL: Me?

ILLY: Yes.

MARSHAL: I'm going great guns, Illy.

ILLY: It's bad luck when you run out of petrol.

MARSHAL: Yes . . . yes . . .

ILLY: How are you, Toby?

TOBY: Fine thanks.

ILLY: Good. Well, I must be off for lunch. Goodbye to you.

[ILLY *goes off towards the road.* MARSHAL *and* TOBY *watch him go.*]

MARSHAL: He's a relentless bastard. He's gunna hang around me like Marley's ghost and remind me what a bastard I am.

TOBY: He probably hopes you'll change your mind and let him have his farm.

MARSHAL: Yeah, well he won't wear me down. Of course, I'm not the only reason he's hanging around, I would hazard.

TOBY: Oh, no?

MARSHAL: Has he ever said to you . . . what about . . .

TOBY: Has he ever asked me for a . . . gosh? The answer, truthfully, is not as such. But I got the impression he wanted to gosh me.

MARSHAL: Yeah, well you watch out for Illy. There's been more than one broken heart and shotgun episode in that little life. Not to mention the lady tourist who jumped ship and then later tried to kill herself.

TOBY: Gosh.

MARSHAL: Illy's an honourable man, but he's not a hundred percent honest. And the ladies' man side of him is a bit of a problem, too. You know, I wonder about ladies' men. I reckon that any bloke who is a ladies' man is a bit suspect.

TOBY: In what sense?

MARSHAL: Well. I just wonder what his concentration span must be like. I mean, for example, if you gave a ladies' man a day's work, would he finish it in a day?

TOBY: You mean they do their best work at night?

MARSHAL: No, Toby. Now look. I'm not trying to be smutty. I'm just speculating; and I'd have to say this. I'd have to say I'd have one or two qualms about putting a ladies' man in charge of the shop. On the other hand, Illy's a typical Indian. He'll work till he drops.

TOBY: What 'shop' are you talking about?

MARSHAL: I'm just being metaphorical.

[TAKA *brings out an orange juice. She looks around for* JAMES. MARSHAL *takes the glass.*]
Thanks. Taka.

[*He drains the glass.*]

TOBY: Marshal, I was thinking, you know, that . . . um . . .

MARSHAL: Come on, Toby, out with it.

TOBY: I was thinking that I wouldn't mind staying on.

MARSHAL: Well, as far as work's concerned if Ellen doesn't pass her post she'll be shipped off to NZ to find a job, so there won't be anyone to teach around here. Taka and I have run our race.

TAKA: You speak for yourself.

[MARSHAL *laughs.*]

TOBY: I was thinking of other children. I was thinking I could become a kind of gypsy lady with an armful of books. I could be a travelling governess. For a while, anyway.

MARSHAL: Well, there might be a few bob in it, but I wouldn't count on it.

TOBY: I was thinking there might be just enough to get by, to buy a tin of bully beef every now and then.

MARSHAL: I'll tell you what. I'll write you a reference and I'll write to a few people and tell them about you and you can see how you go from there. All right?

TOBY: That would be wonderful.

MARSHAL: But you know, Toby, we can't stay here for ever, we'll have to get out eventually, us whites. Won't we, Taka?

TAKA: You will pay your bills first, I hope.

[MARSHAL *laughs.*]

TOBY: When do you think Fiji will become independent?

MARSHAL: When it grows up. Well, I'd better get this petrol back to the car. Bloody petrol gauge must be broken.

TOBY: [*soothingly*] They're not built to last.

MARSHAL: That is what I want to hear. See you later.

[MARSHAL *has filled his container with petrol from the bowser and goes off towards the road with the container.*]

TAKA: That would be very good for you, very good if Marshal writes the letters. He is well respected in Fiji. It will be very good for you.

TOBY: Yes. Let's hope so. Thanks for the thought, Taka.

TAKA: Why are you so keen to stay?

TOBY: I like it here, and I don't think I'd like to go back home. Most of the people I know there have settled down for the run to the judge. They don't laugh and they don't cry. And those who do are fruitcakes. I'm better off here. I'm better off alive.

TAKA: Perhaps you will meet a nice young, a nice Field Officer, and settle down.

TOBY: I doubt it, Taka. The prospect of becoming a Field Officer's wife doesn't grip, it doesn't sustain. Even if the Field Office were on the other side of the island from someone as accident-prone as Mr Ram, I can't see myself handling the day-to-day, year upon year practicalities of such a life. And a life such as that would find me wanting.

TAKA: Then what will you do?

TOBY: Exist. Exist here for as long as I can. Perhaps educate. Encourage. Inspire... well, perhaps not. But I can educate and encourage. And that can't be bad.

TAKA: Then be a good girl and you may do well.

TOBY: You shouldn't have told me that, Taka.

TAKA: Why?

TOBY: I have a tendency to self-destruct.

TAKA: You want to destroy yourself?

TOBY: Not exactly. But to an old bohemian like me the challenge is to do the wrong thing and get away with it.

TAKA: Don't go out with Illy. Get your reference.

TOBY: Why should I?

TAKA: You seem to me to be someone who has lived a bit wild at times, but now it is time to be ...

TOBY: Tame? You think I should be tame?

TAKA: Perhaps not tame.

TOBY: Wise?

TAKA: Not quite.

TOBY: Smart?

TAKA: Yes.

TOBY: Gosh. There I feel the job is well and truly in front of me. About infinity miles in front of me.

TAKA: That's all I can say. Your lunch is ready.

[TAKA *goes inside leaving a pensive* TOBY. *Lights remain on* TOBY *and fade out elsewhere.*

TOBY *picks up a drink from the table on the verandah. Lights up everywhere.* TOBY *paces up and down the verandah. A bottle of whisky, some other bottles and some ice are on the table.*

It is a few days later, early in the evening. MARSHAL *comes out on to the verandah, holding a pre-dinner drink.*]

MARSHAL: Aha. Here's the lady with the problem.

TOBY: What problem?

MARSHAL: I don't know. You look like a lady with a problem.

TOBY: I feel fine.

MARSHAL: I'll get around to writing those letters for you this weekend. I've been a bit busy the last couple of days. Changes in company policy to be implemented, etcetera.

TOBY: I understand.

MARSHAL: I'm surprised to see that you're a lady alone with a problem. I would've thought you'd have your work cut out warding off young Jim, for one.

TOBY: We've been out a couple of times, but he's a bit hot and cold. We seem to have missed.

MARSHAL: A lot of Poms are like that. It's the winters they have to live through. They're all cooped up indoors for far too long. That's my theory, anyway.

TOBY: Are you thinking of recommending Jimmy for that marginal land?

MARSHAL: My first choice would be someone from the valley, like Ram junior. But if he's going to stay on and study badminton at the University of Madras then I'll have to think again. I haven't made up my mind about Jimmy. I can't decide whether he's one of those types we get breezing through here from time to time with big schemes that never work, or whether he's fair dinkum.

TOBY: He's only made the short list because he's related to a friend of yours. Is that right?

MARSHAL: That's the way it goes. After all, how did you come to be here?

TOBY: I didn't think it was charity alone.

MARSHAL: Now just calm down, Toby. Do you think for one minute that I would give the nod — for what it's worth — to Jimmy just because of some kind of old boy network? No. Not now. Not ever. Jimmy is one of the most capable blokes I have ever met. He's done a few jobs for me around the valley and I tell you he's so capable he's almost too good to be true. That's the only thing that worries me about him.

> [JAMES *comes out of the house, fairly blearily.* MARSHAL *considers him.*]

JAMES: Evening, Marshal. Toby.

MARSHAL: Have you just got up?

JAMES: Yes.

MARSHAL: Most people do their sleeping at night.

JAMES: Yes, I know, Marshal. I know. It's awful. I just find the atmosphere too thick, too steamy. I find it's difficult to breathe. And when you do, you find it's by no means a sure thing that the air's going to reach your lungs. And then there's the corollary: why breathe? I mean, what do you do here? You cut cane and you drink beer. The women are well below par — savin' your presence, mum. The food's pretty unmemorable and, well, the opportunities for a bright young chap — that's me, by the way — are a bit limited. I might push off to Rhodesia and try my luck there. I mean, you know, it's not as if anyone's come up with anything concrete while I've been here.

MARSHAL: No one comes up with anything concrete anywhere.

JAMES: Yes. Well. I might go and tuck into the yams. Are the yams on tonight? Or is it seaweed again?

MARSHAL: It's yams.

JAMES: Marvellous. Excuse me.

> [*He goes.*]

MARSHAL: Looks like Ram junior's the pea.

TOBY: Not Illy?

MARSHAL: Not Illy.

TOBY: That's a pity. I'd like you two to get on better.

MARSHAL: Oh yes?

TOBY: I'm going out with Illy tonight.

MARSHAL: [*stunned*] Oh yes?

TOBY: We're going to a carnival in Sigatoka. Magicians and things.

MARSHAL: You're not.

TOBY: Yes.

MARSHAL: They'll be all Indians there.

TOBY: That's all right.

MARSHAL: Speaks English to you, does he?

TOBY: Yes, he speaks English.

MARSHAL: It's a long way to Sigatoka. We'll leave a light on for you.

TOBY: You don't approve, do you?

MARSHAL: No.

TOBY: Why don't you approve?

MARSHAL: We're living on the fringe here. This is where our way of life ends and theirs begins. It's not 'anything goes' here. If it's 'anything goes' then we may well go. And there wouldn't be too much cane being cut. Look, Toby. It's not as if there are a million bloody rules for whites living in the Pacific. There are only a few. And it doesn't hurt to observe them.

TOBY: I don't see what rule I've broken.

MARSHAL: What you do in private. Doesn't matter. But the black man/white woman double is definitely not the go in public. They frown on Illy and Taka being together because he's Indian and she's Fijian. What do you think they'll say when they see you and Illy — who is notorious anyway — out on the town together? What do you think your reputation will be worth?

TOBY: I don't care. We're going out together.

MARSHAL: What would Billy say? I don't know. Girls like you, middle class girls, you always do the same thing. You pick the very bloke who's going to destroy you. Billy would have a fit. He'd say you're old enough to know better. I would have thought that you, above all you, would know better. This is the nineteen-fifties. You play golf. You've travelled. Billy would shoot himself.

TOBY: If I'd wanted to destroy myself I would have stayed

where I was.

[PHILIP *comes in from the road carrying a letter.*]

PHILIP: Marshal.

MARSHAL: What is it?

PHILIP: It's a letter from my father.

MARSHAL: Give it here.

[MARSHAL *snatches the letter and goes inside.*]

PHILIP: Great stuff, Marshal. Has he been rubbishing you too?

TOBY: No. I'm just seasonally depressed.

PHILIP: Can I get you anything?

TOBY: Thank you, Philip dear. I'll have a whisky and soda.

PHILIP: With ice?

TOBY: You bet. I need Dutch courage and coolness.

[PHILIP *makes her a drink at the table.*]

PHILIP: What's the matter? Are you in trouble?

TOBY: I just had an argument with Marshal.

PHILIP: I'm not surprised. Marshal's so. . .I don't know. . . insensitive. . .crass. . .

TOBY: What's he done to you?

PHILIP: Oh, nothing in particular. It's just him. Everything he does. At the cricket he was drinking beer at eleven a.m. and wearing red socks.

TOBY: Dear me.

PHILIP: Well, what kind of Cyril wears red socks for cricket? And he said to this woman whose husband was away 'I'll have to come round and deliver your ice.'

TOBY: Now Philip, that's just a pleasantry.

PHILIP: But she was an old bag.

TOBY: Then it was gallantry. Some of us do have to get old, you know.

PHILIP: Okay, so maybe that was a bad example. You can shoot down everything I say. But you can't deny he's corny and crass and he just doesn't notice anything. My father's the same. He's a buffoon and he doesn't understand a thing. Okay, so he understands some things. But *I* don't want to end up like that.

TOBY: Now Philip. You're a sensitive boy. You're a serious boy. The trick for you would be to grow up without

turning bitter. If you do you'll realise that Marshal is a
very sharp man. I know he sounds a bit corny, but so
what? He enjoys his beer and his little jokes and he enjoys
life more than most. He's certainly sharper than you or I
will ever be.

PHILIP: Sharp? His mind's gone. He's nearly senile.

TOBY: Now you listen to me. Marshal is a very good man.
There are a *lot* worse than him. He's had to work hard
and perhaps that's made him seem a bit, I don't know, a
bit crude? He might seem a bit crude to you but he's a
very fair man and a good man and if you can't give him
your respect now you will when you get a bit older. And
when you get a bit older you'll see, what, the, I don't know,
the choices? The choices Marshal's had to make, the
choices in his life, the choices for others under his care,
and you'll see what he had to do and you'll hope you can
do as well. And be as good a man.

PHILIP: Yeah, well I hope . . . I can . . .

[*He approaches her.*]

TOBY: Hey. Hey. You just sit down for a minute.

PHILIP: I just wanted to kiss you. I think you're wonderful.

TOBY: You just sit down. I've had enough on my plate
recently in that field of human endeavour.

PHILIP: I don't care. I think you're like something out of
heaven.

[*He takes her arm. She disengages herself along the
verandah.*]

TOBY: Um. Look. Philip. I don't know what kind of ideal
you think you're building up but I think you should look
at the facts. I'm in my thirties, fairly irrevocably now, and
I may be a bloody good-looker, but I'm just a person, just
ticking over, having a reasonable time, waiting eventually
for the Reaper. I'm not some idol. I'm not your mother
and I won't be your lover. You won't be offended, will
you?

PHILIP: I won't lay a finger on you ever again.

TOBY: Well. Um. I didn't mind that so much.

[*He kisses her. She disengages.*]

But I thought. . . well, you should know that I'm nothing

much.

PHILIP: Oh, sure. You're nothing much.

TOBY: The point I'm making, Philip, is that I feel you've underestimated Marshal and overestimated me.

PHILIP: I wonder why.

TOBY: When you finally grow up, Philip, you'll realise that life is people like Marshal. That's what it's all about, red socks or no. And you'll realise that there are a lot worse Marshals than Marshal. I think he's a wonderful man. He's sometimes harsh in his judgements and stubborn when it comes to what he calls 'the rules', but he knows how to keep control. And that's what you have to do when you're living on the margin as we all do here.

[*The headlights of* ILLY's *car sweep across the front of the house.* TOBY *turns and looks down the road. The noise of* ILLY's *car cuts out.*]

And when you're living on the very edge of the margin it's more imperative still that you have strength and just perhaps a touch of bastardry.

[ILLY *comes in from the road.* TOBY *goes out purposefully to meet him and puts her arms around him without hesitation.*]

It's good to see you.

[*She kisses him.* PHILIP *stares at them.*]

You know Philip, don't you?

ILLY: Yes.

TOBY: You smell nice.

ILLY: Duty free cologne.

[MARSHAL *comes out on to the verandah, followed by* ELLEN *and* TAKA. TOBY *faces them.*]

TOBY: We're going to Sigatoka and we're going in a borrowed car. I hope no one minds.

[MARSHAL, ELLEN *and* TAKA *look steadily at her.*]

Good night, then. Good night to you all.

[*She turns and leads* ILLY *towards the road.*]

MARSHAL: Ay, Illy.

ILLY: [*turning*] Yes.

MARSHAL: Got enough petrol?

[ILLY *grins.*]

ILLY: I have just the right amount.

> [TOBY *is disturbed for a moment, but then realises*
> MARSHAL *is just trying to ease the tension. She*
> *manages a grim smile. So does* MARSHAL.]

Come on.

> [ILLY *leads* TOBY *out. The others stand still, watching*
> *them go. The lights fade on everyone except* MARSHAL
> *while the others go.*
>
> MARSHAL *takes out a letter and reads it. The lights*
> *turn to daylight, a few weeks later.*
>
> *He folds the letter and puts it on the table, picks up*
> *the soda siphon and squirts some soda water on his*
> *face.* TAKA *brings him a pannikin of kava, which he*
> *downs. Then he squirts some soda down his throat.*
> TAKA *waits.*]

MARSHAL: What is it, Taka?

TAKA: The boy from Ram's was up this morning.

MARSHAL: Ohr no!

TAKA: It seems there is trouble with the railway gang. The tracks are not being cleared.

MARSHAL: What sort of trouble?

TAKA: I believe it's a strike of some kind.

> [ILLY *enters from the road. He carries a piece of paper*
> *in one hand and a chicken coop with two small*
> *chickens in the other.*]

MARSHAL: Hello, Illy. You look very militant this morning.

ILLY: They're a present from Ram on the Nadi road.

> [TAKA *takes the coop and goes.*]

MARSHAL: So, Illy. Trouble on the railways, eh?

ILLY: Yes.

MARSHAL: Why've they sent you?

ILLY: I'm the new sirdah.

MARSHAL: Yes, I heard there'd been a bit of a coup in the upper reaches of the railway gang fraternity. But why'd they pick you?

> [ILLY *shrugs.*]

ILLY: No religious ties. No enemies.

MARSHAL: You mean there was no one there whose sister or wife you haven't knocked off?

ILLY: I had no *religious* enemies.

MARSHAL: And that piece of paper contains your demands, I suppose.

ILLY: Starting with a forty-hour week.

MARSHAL: I never pictured you as a keen trade unionist, Illy.

ILLY: Nevertheless, you're going to have a strike on your hands.

MARSHAL: Illy, you've probably heard on the bush telegraph that there are changes coming in company policy and probably a change in the name of the company. More and more of the work is going to be turned over to locals. It's partly a sense of inevitability, partly because of the activities of people such as your good self.

ILLY: Oh, yes.

MARSHAL: Maybe not you personally, Illy. You're not the greatest political organiser of the century. You're far more concerned with. . .

ILLY: Selfish ends?

MARSHAL: Yes.

ILLY: You know what I want, Marshal. I want my due.

MARSHAL: Yes. Illy, in many ways you're as straight as an arrow, but I just can't quite get over the fact that you've done a bit of thieving here and there.

ILLY: Not thieving. I've taken *back* things.

MARSHAL: That's a bit inadequate, Illy. That's a bit Petty Sessions.

ILLY: It's part of my due.

MARSHAL: Yes. I suppose, really, it's a question of perspective.

ILLY: Sure. Now. We've got business to do.

MARSHAL: We sure have. How'd you like to take my place as the Field Officer here?

[ILLY *is amazed, but quickly recovers.*]

ILLY: Does the house go with it?

MARSHAL: And the shed.

ILLY: I'll take it.

MARSHAL: Good. Of course it's not my final decision, but my recommendation will be pretty conclusive. And I'm going to recommend you because you haven't got anyone in the valley you could favour on racial or religious grounds. As well as that you're bright and you work hard and you're capable all round.

ILLY: When do I start?

MARSHAL: You'll have to undergo a training course, either here or in Queensland and you'll have to satisfy the company you'll do a good job.

ILLY: [*dubiously*] Oh, yes.

MARSHAL: You'll walk it in, Illy. So are we agreed?

ILLY: [*swiftly making up his mind*] Yes.

MARSHAL: [*holding up* ILLY's *piece of paper*] Good. Now what do we do about these demands?

ILLY: The demands stand.

MARSHAL: Okay. Will you have a drink on it?

ILLY: Yes. I'll have a drink.

MARSHAL: [*grinning*] You're a bastard, Illy. You are a bastard. [*Calling into the house*] Taka! Taka! [*Considering* ILLY] How are you going to handle it Illy? The whole Toby angle. And your new job with CSR.

ILLY: I don't know.

MARSHAL: My advice to you is forget about the Takas and the Tobys and either get married to an *Indian* girl or walk into a pencil sharpener.

[TAKA *brings out the kava.*]

ILLY: I don't agree.

MARSHAL: You can trace all trouble back to a migration or a boundary being crossed. Ideally, you should go to India.

ILLY: We are strangers in India.

MARSHAL: I'm not suggesting you go there, Illy. I'm being hypothetical, abstract. I'm just saying your path won't always be smooth.

ILLY: I have had my moments of pleasure.

[TAKA *goes back into the house.*]

If I wanted to marry Toby, would they try to sack me as Field Officer?

MARSHAL: No. But they wouldn't be happy and you probably wouldn't get too much further in the company.

[ILLY *digests this.* TOBY *comes in from the road, holding hands with* PHILIP *and* ELLEN. *They are all bright and happy.*]

TOBY: You see. I told you the verandah would still be here when we got back.

PHILIP: Yes, well I didn't doubt that, Toby.

ELLEN: It was the way it looked that counted.

TOBY: If you'd done badly how would it have looked?

PHILIP: Like a scaffold.

ELLEN: It would have been dark.

TOBY: But now it looks like gingerbread in the sunlight, is that correct?

PHILIP: Could be.

ELLEN: Yes, it does.

TOBY: Except for those two shockers throwing shadows.

MARSHAL: How'd it go, Ellen?

ELLEN: Won-n-nderful! I'm sure I passed with As and Honours and everything nice. I feel I could skip over the sea on a day like this. No more pencils, no more books, no more teachers' — now don't get upset.

TOBY: I won't get upset. I'll just stand back and look at my two happy children. No I won't, I'll look at them up close.
    [*She grabs* PHILIP *and .*ELLEN *and hugs them, then releases them.*]
You're right. No more teachers. This is the end of the road. No response to my letters. Nobody wants an old governess.

PHILIP: We don't want you to go immediately.

TOBY: Dear Philip! Thank you. Well, Marshal, the exams are finished, I'm sure they passed, and just look at them. Don't they look relieved? They look to me as if they passed.

MARSHAL: By gee, you know, Toby, when I look at those youngsters and the smiles on their faces, I say to myself, 'By gee that Toby's unplugged them both'. What a pity it's all over now.

TOBY: They'll always be my children. My children.

MARSHAL: They surely will, Toby.

ILLY: What will you do now?

[TOBY *looks at* ILLY *sharply. She is slightly wounded but she quickly recovers.*]

TOBY: You're interested, are you? Well then, I can tell you this. I think I will reflect awhile. On my past and present. And I think I will a wee drop take. But enough of me. For at least a minute. I want to know about you. I don't see tufts of Marshal's hair in your fist. I see signs of chumminess, albeit with all proper reserve.

ILLY: This is as chummy as you'll ever see us.

MARSHAL: Now, Illy. I've always nursed a deep feeling of warmth towards you.

ILLY: It's the kava talking.

MARSHAL: My only reservations were engendered by one or two flaws in your character that I was not too ecstatic about.

ILLY: You can retire happy, Marshal, knowing you were the last Field Officer to be a perfect human being.

TOBY: Retire?

MARSHAL: Yes. I'd like you to meet my successor, the new hope of CSR.

TOBY: Illy?

MARSHAL: None other. I offered him my job and he accepted.

[TOBY *stares at them.* JAMES *comes out on to the verandah.*]

JAMES: Hello hello hello. *And*. Goodbye goodbye goodbye. More of the latter, in fact. I'm leaving today.

MARSHAL: Now that saddens me. I didn't think you were chooffing off till next week.

JAMES: Alas. Time marches on. This *is* next week.

MARSHAL: By jees, you're right. This *is* next week.

JAMES: Exactly.

MARSHAL: So where is it you're going?

JAMES: Auckland first, and from there I'll push off to Salisbury, I think. Depends. There's an old pal of mine runs a charter service in the South Island. Might give him a call. See if he needs a bright young chap. In which case I would be the bright young chap who would do a bloody good job.

TOBY: I hope you stay in the South Island.

JAMES: Why, are you planning a visit to Salisbury?

TOBY: Oh, Jimmy. You've been good to me. I wish I'd known you were going, I'd have got you a present.

JAMES: Just give me a kiss.

[*She kisses him.*]

TOBY: Jimmy, will you be all right?

[JAMES *laughs.*]

JAMES: I'll keep the guillotine at bay.

TOBY: You were so good to me when I arrived and I'll never forget it. I hope you stay in the South Island or somewhere in this part of the world. Please let me know if you do.

JAMES: Sure. I'll drop you a postcard.

TOBY: I'll come and visit you.

JAMES: Sure.

TOBY: I mean it, Jimmy. I'll visit you.

JAMES: It'd be lovely to see you, of course. But Toby, I intend to give the local talent a warm reception if and when I get there.

TOBY: You'll be pleased to see me, I promise. I'll visit you and we'll have a great time together.

JAMES: Marvellous. But where will you be coming from?

TOBY: Somewhere in this part of the world.

[JAMES *looks at her keenly for a moment, wondering how she will end up.*]

JAMES: Now. Time for a few goodbyes. Marshal.

MARSHAL: Good luck, Jimmy.

JAMES: Thanks beyond repair. I mean, just fantastic. Hope I can repay you.

MARSHAL: She's right, Jimmy. And thanks for *your* help.

JAMES: Goodbye, Illy.

ILLY: Yes, Jim.

[*They shake hands.*]

JAMES: And Philip. About time you started to enjoy yourself, don't you think?

PHILIP: I have and I will.

JAMES: I do believe he means it.

PHILIP: All the best, Jim. And good luck, too.

[*They shake hands.*]

JAMES: Thanks. And Little Orphan Ellen.

[ELLEN *is crying.*]

ELLEN: Oh, Jimmy.

JAMES: Hey. Where's my favourite tough girl?

ELLEN: Please don't go.

JAMES: Come on. I'll see you again. On South Island or downtown Salisbury. I'll see you again. And you'll be old enough then for me to take you out on the town.

ELLEN: Jimmy, I . . .

JAMES: Yes.

ELLEN: I just think you're wonderful.

JAMES: Goodbye, darling girl. You get your guard up next time you see me.

ELLEN: No, I won't.

[*She hugs him. He gradually disengages.*]

JAMES: And Toby.

[*They kiss lightly.*]

TOBY: I'll be there.

[JAMES *smiles and looks around.*]

JAMES: Goodbye, everyone.

MARSHAL: What about your luggage?

JAMES: I looked around all my gear and, do you know, there wasn't a thing I wanted to keep? Cheerio.

[*He goes out to the road.* ELLEN *runs out after him.*]

MARSHAL: We get a few of those through here.

TOBY: A few of what? I assume you mean handsome pilots who ought to be shanghaied by any woman with sense.

MARSHAL: Poms who flame out in the tropics.

TOBY: Jimmy did not flame out. He just found things a bit inadequate.

MARSHAL: I'm not bagging him. He was a good bloke. Like my good mate Illy here.

ILLY: [*grinning*] Now, Marshal.

MARSHAL: I don't mind telling you I've taken to this gurkha. I think he's terrific.

ILLY: Get out of it, you old bastard.

[MARSHAL *laughs.*]

TOBY: Illy. A Field Officer with CSR. How on earth did

that happen?

MARSHAL: Illy was propelling himself into an unfamiliar role — that of a union leader of the militant variety — so I ended his brief career by offering him my job of Field Officer.

[TOBY *turns to* PHILIP, *indicating* MARSHAL.]

TOBY: Sharp.

PHILIP: [*smiling*] Shar*pish*.

TOBY: But what about you, Marshal? What will you do? Now that Ellen's heading for the mainland.

MARSHAL: Well, I, er, don't know if you're cognisant with the fact that I've been keeping company with an NZ lass in Lautoka, but it just might happen that I might shoot off to NZ with this particular lass.

ILLY: Young love, is it, Marshal?

MARSHAL: Now, don't have a shot at me. We'll do very nicely. And so will you, if you work hard. By the way, you'll need these to do my job.

[*He flips a small packet to* ILLY, *who catches it.* MARSHAL *turns to* TOBY *and explains.*]

Aspirins.

ILLY: I'll handle it. I've got it up here.

MARSHAL: Sure you have.

ILLY: And with Toby to help me I'll be unstoppable.

TOBY: Eh?

ILLY: Will you marry me?

[TOBY *tries to sort this out.*]

TOBY: [*swallowing hard*] This is a tiny bit public, isn't it?

ILLY: In front of witnesses I want to say this, so there's no mistake. I love you and I want to marry you. I don't care who knows. And I don't care what the consequences are.

TOBY: Let me think about that. I'm not brave like you. Let me run away and think about that.

[*She jumps up on to the verandah, then turns at the door.*]

Will you all excuse me while I go and break down irretrievably? There are one or two things I have to think about, and it always helps to break down irretrievably. Good morning, good afternoon and good night.

[*She disappears into the house. The others look after her.*

MARSHAL approaches ILLY, who stands next to him. He takes the aspirins.]

MARSHAL: Bad move.

[*MARSHAL goes into the house. ILLY turns and goes to the edge of the verandah. He looks out over the valley. PHILIP turns and looks at him. Fade on everything except ILLY. PHILIP goes.*

TAKA comes out of the house and takes off ILLY's shirt. She ties some padding around his stomach, then she puts a different shirt on him. She hands him a drink and goes.

Lights up everywhere else. It is late in the afternoon, a few years later.

ILLY sips his drink, looking out over the valley. TAKA comes out of the house.]

TAKA: There'll be a visitor this evening.

ILLY: I know.

TAKA: Not her. Ellen.

ILLY: Ellen?

TAKA: You remember. Marshal's daughter.

ILLY: Oh, yes.

TAKA: She must be twenty-two or so now. She's an airline stewardess, but she's leaving to have a baby. This is her last flight through Nadi so she's coming up to see us.

ILLY: Ellen. She'll get a shock.

TAKA: So will we. I'll say hello to her and then goodbye. I'll be back on Monday night.

ILLY: Monday night.

TAKA: [*firmly*] At the earliest.

ILLY: Okay.

TAKA: You can live with that?

ILLY: Live without it, you mean.

TAKA: You will survive, my love.

[*She smiles and gives him a quick kiss. ELLEN, now a relaxed and attractive young woman, comes in from the road. She looks at the house for a moment.*]

TAKA: Ellen! Is it Ellen?

ELLEN: Yes, it's me, Taka.

TAKA: Look at you. Look at you. You're such a young lady now. [*She hugs* ELLEN.]

ELLEN: You look just the same, Taka.

TAKA: Oh yes, I never change. And life goes on. Who do you think this is, this lord of the manor?

ELLEN: Hello, Illy.

ILLY: Welcome back, Ellen.

ELLEN: Thank you. Where's Toby?

TAKA: Oh, she'll be along.

ILLY: She comes up for the weekends.

TAKA: Yes.

ELLEN: And what about you, Illy? Still with CSR?

ILLY: Not CSR any more. We're had a name change. Now it's South Pacific Sugar Mills and I'm a Field Officer. I give my heart and soul to SPSM and they give me a good living wage. It's an arrangement that's not perfect. But it will do. Where's Philip these days?

ELLEN: Philip? Oh, he's working hard. He's in Hong Kong and with an electronics company or something. He's engaged.

ILLY: Do you see much of him?

ELLEN: No.

[*Lights flicker in from the road.*]

TAKA: That's Toby's car now.

ELLEN: I'm so excited. I can't wait to see her. She was my heroine, looking back on it. She had such guts, and what heart. And style, too.

[ILLY *and* TAKA *exchange glances.*]

ILLY: She's. . .still a lovely woman.

TAKA: It has been hard for her.

ELLEN: What's been hard?

TAKA: Here she is now.

[TOBY *comes in from the road. She wears highly coloured clothes, a shawl, and large earrings. Fiji has not been kind to her complexion. She carries a basket.*
ELLEN *turns and stares at her as she approaches.*]

TOBY: What's this? A new model, is it? A new model for Illy?

TAKA: It's Ellen. She's come to pay us a visit.

TOBY: Ellen! Well. What a young lady.

ELLEN: Hello, Toby.

> [*She stands staring at* TOBY.]

TOBY: Well, it's young Ellen come back. We're all getting on a bit, you know. Taka and Illy and I, we're all hurtling along, towards oblivion, like those sputnik-type things in space.

ILLY: Vostok-type things.

TOBY: All right. Vostoks. Who cares out here on the frontier? This is primary industry first and last around here.

ILLY: Well put. She puts things well.

TOBY: What have we got for young Ellen? Let's have a look and see what we've got for young Ellen.

> [*She burrows into her basket and comes up with an apple.*]

Have an apple, dear. An apple from your old teacher.

ELLEN: No thanks. I've just eaten.

> [TOBY *takes a bite out of the apple and chews it, then drops the apple absently back in the basket.*]

TOBY: So you've come to visit, eh?

ELLEN: Yes.

TOBY: Well here we are.

TAKA: I must go, Ellen. You come any time. This is always your home.

ELLEN: Thank you, Taka.

TAKA: And I'll see you.

> [*She kisses* ILLY.]

Goodbye, Toby.

> [TAKA *goes.* TOBY *considers* ELLEN.]

TOBY: So you've come back to see us. I think that's very nice.

ELLEN: I came back to tell you something too.

TOBY: Oh, and what have you got to tell us?

ELLEN: That. . .I'll always be grateful to you. You brought me over the hill. When I was a struggling teenager you brought me over the hill.

TOBY: Oow, it was nothing. No-thing. I was happy to be able to help out. But it's all different now, Ellen dear. Oh yes. It's all different now. I think that, quick as a wink, and equally quietly, and with nobody there to see or push, I think that Illy and I, while nobody was looking, Illy and I might have just gone over the hill ourselves. Illy, I think, is certainly over the hill — look at the weight he's put on.

ILLY: What are you doing, Ellen? You listening to this old crone?

TOBY: Ooh, did you hear that? Now he's putting the boot in. I think he wants to get rid of me.

ILLY: That will be the day.

TOBY: You mean you want to keep on with me?

ILLY: Oh, I think so, yes. We've each had our chances but now I think we're stuck. And that is not too bad when you consider that I'm rather fond of this old crone.

[TOBY *cackles*.]

TOBY: Ooh, you hear that, Ellen? You hear that? He's after me again, I can tell.

ILLY: The only thing that turns me off is when I hear that chicken-cackle.

[TOBY *cackles*.]

TOBY: It brings him on like nothing on earth, I can tell you.

ELLEN: It's nice to see. . . affection between you still, after all these years.

TOBY: Oh, there's affection — and more. Sometimes he rings me up in the middle of the week and says 'Come up and see me'. And I have to tell him that no, I've got to keep the shop open during the week. Besides, he's got Taka from Monday to Friday. But of course, you know, sometimes I give in and I come up in the middle of the week. Sometimes we sit out here and drink a bit of kava and we talk about things, sometimes even about you and Philip, and we watch the sun set, and I'd have to admit it's as good a way of spending the middle of the week as any I know. Of course, being a dress shop lady, I'm too busy to do it more often, but it's nice to know that it's there. What's the matter with you?

[ELLEN *is crying*.]

ELLEN: Oh, Toby! Oh no!

[*She runs out to the road.*]

TOBY: What was that all about?

ILLY: Never mind. Never mind.

TOBY: Was I being rude?

ILLY: No, Toby.

TOBY: It must have been something I did or said. Or maybe. Maybe it was the sight of me. Maybe that poor little girl came back to see someone exceptional. And what did she see? She saw me. Maybe it was the sight of me that drove her off. The sheer sight of me.

ILLY: No. No. Forget it. Look, there was something I wanted to ask you. Why not stay Sunday night as well? That would give us three nights out of seven. You'd get back easily on Monday morning.

[TOBY *considers* ILLY.]

TOBY: I can read you like a book, Iqbal Ilyas. Now that Taka's getting married, you're worried about getting your oats.

ILLY: That's it.

TOBY: Well, if I want to beat you off with a stick, I will.

ILLY: You do that.

TOBY: Unless of course the real reason you want me for an extra night is because you need my company.

ILLY: That could be.

TOBY: I can read you like a book, Mr Iqbal Ilyas the Third.

ILLY: Come on, we'll go and have some dinner.

[*He assists her across the verandah. She stops.*]

TOBY: What *do* you suppose got Ellen so upset?

ILLY: This is her old house. She suffered a pang of the heart.

[TOBY *looks around in a sweep and then stops.*]

TOBY: Of course. She'll be back tomorrow, in the daylight.

ILLY: Of course. Now let's go in and eat.

TOBY: They were both my children, you know.

ILLY: Yes, Toby. But now it's time to go.

[*He escorts her into the house. Fade out.*]

THE END